ACOUSTIC GUITAR MAGAZINE'S
private lessons

ACOUSTIC GUITAR SOLO FINGERSTYLE BASICS

STRING LETTER PUBLISHING

Publisher: David A. Lusterman

Series Editor: Jeffrey Pepper Rodgers

Editors: Andrew DuBrock and Stacey Lynn

Music Editing and Audio Production: Andrew DuBrock

Music Transcriptions and Engraving: Andrew DuBrock

Designer: Gary Cribb

Production Director: Ellen Richman

Production Designer: Susan Pinkerton

Marketing Manager: Jennifer Fujimoto

Licensing: Joan Murray

Cover Photo: Rory Earnshaw

Photographs: Aimee Strathman (Andrew DuBrock), Pat Mann
(Ken Perlman), Ben Ailes (Dale Miller), Happy Traum
(Al Petteway), Mike Huibregtse (Mark Hanson), Paul Miholland
(Gary Joyner)

Printed in the United States of America.
All rights reserved. This book was produced by String Letter Publishing, Inc.
PO Box 767, San Anselmo, California 94979-0767
(415) 485-6946; www.acousticguitar.com

STRING LETTER PUBLISHING

contents

CD track list

introduction

What is fingerstyle guitar? Everyone plays guitar with their fingers, whether they use the ones on their left hand to fret notes or the ones on their right hand to strum or pick. So the term *fingerstyle* may seem misleading. Fingerstyle guitar can include any number of "styles," from modern classical to Celtic to jazz. What ties these forms together in the fingerstyle realm is the use of your right-hand fingers to slap, pick, thwack, and pluck out patterns on the strings of the guitar.

This book takes a look at many different styles of music, all from a fingerstyle perspective. You'll learn how to thump out country blues bass lines like Big Bill Broonzy, arrange Celtic tunes originally played on harp, and even pick up a few classical exercises from the masters. Eight in-depth lessons from teachers of many styles will help you get a better grasp on fingerstyle music, which, as you can see, is an incredibly versatile approach to the guitar. And, since a good portion of fingerstyle guitar involves playing solo songs, this book should leave you primed to enter the world of solo fingerstyle performance.

If you're unfamiliar with the terms or techniques used in the lessons, be sure to check the music notation key on page 6. If you're ready to go, dive in!

Andrew DuBrock
Music Editor
Acoustic Guitar magazine

music notation key

The music in this book is written in standard notation and tablature. Here's how to read it.

STANDARD NOTATION

Standard notation is written on a five-line staff. Notes are written in alphabetical order from A to G.

The duration of a note is determined by three things: the note head, stem, and flag. A whole note (○) equals four beats. A half note (♩) is half of that: two beats. A quarter note (♩) equals one beat, an eighth note (♪) equals half of one beat, and a 16th note (♬) is a quarter beat (there are four 16th notes per beat).

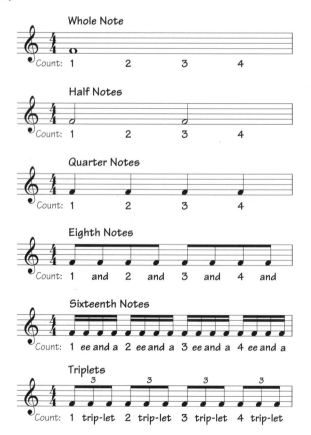

The fraction (4/4, 3/4, 6/8, etc.) or ¢ character shown at the beginning of a piece of music denotes the time signature. The top number tells you how many beats are in each measure, and the bottom number indicates the rhythmic value of each beat (4 equals a quarter note, 8 equals an eighth note, 16 equals a 16th note, and 2 equals a half note). The most common time signature is 4/4, which signifies four quarter notes per measure and is sometimes designated with the symbol ¢ (for common time). The symbol ¢ stands for cut time (2/2). Most songs are either in 4/4 or 3/4.

TABLATURE

In tablature, the six horizontal lines represent the six strings of the guitar, with the first string on the top and sixth on the bottom. The numbers refer to fret numbers on a given string. The notation and tablature in this book are designed to be used in tandem—refer to the notation to get the rhythmic information and note durations, and refer to the tablature to get the exact locations of the notes on the guitar fingerboard.

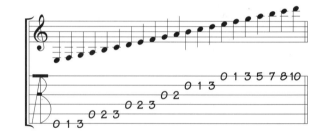

FINGERINGS

Fingerings are indicated with small numbers and letters in the notation. Fretting-hand fingering is indicated with 1 for the index finger, 2 the middle, 3 the ring, 4 the pinky, and *T* the thumb. Picking-hand fingering is indicated by *i* for the index finger, *m* the middle, *a* the ring, *c* the pinky, and *p* the thumb. Circled numbers indicate the string the note is played on. Remember that the fingerings indicated are only suggestions; if you find a different way that works better for you, use it.

CHORD DIAGRAMS

Chord diagrams show where the fingers go on the fingerboard. Frets are shown horizontally. The thick top line represents the nut. A Roman numeral to the right of a diagram indicates a chord played higher up the neck (in this case the top horizontal line is thin). Strings are shown as vertical lines. The line on the far left represents the sixth (lowest) string, and the line on the far right represents the first (highest) string. Dots show where the fingers go, and thick horizontal lines indicate barres. Numbers above the diagram are left-hand finger numbers, as used in standard notation. Again, the fingerings are only suggestions. An *X* indicates a string that should be muted or not played; 0 indicates an open string.

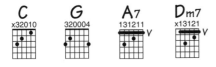

CAPOS

If a capo is used, a Roman numeral indicates the fret where the capo should be placed. The standard notation and tablature is written as if the capo were the nut of the guitar. For instance, a tune capoed anywhere up the neck and played using key-of-G chord shapes and fingerings will be written in the key of G. Likewise, open strings held down by the capo are written as open strings.

TUNINGS

Alternate guitar tunings are given from the lowest (sixth) string to the highest (first) string. For instance, D A D G B E indicates standard tuning with the bottom string dropped to D. Standard notation for songs in alternate tunings always reflects the actual pitches of the notes. Arrows underneath tuning notes indicate strings that are altered from standard tuning and whether they are tuned up or down.

VOCAL TUNES

Vocal tunes are sometimes written with a fully tabbed-out introduction and a vocal melody with chord diagrams for the rest of the piece. The tab intro is usually your indication of which strum or fingerpicking pattern to use in the rest of the piece. The melody with lyrics underneath is the melody sung by the vocalist. Occasionally, smaller notes are written with the melody to indicate the harmony part sung by another vocalist. These are not to be confused with cue notes, which are small notes that indicate melodies that vary when a section is repeated. Listen to a recording of the piece to get a feel for the guitar accompaniment and to hear the singing if you aren't skilled at reading vocal melodies.

ARTICULATIONS

There are a number of ways you can articulate a note on the guitar. Notes connected with slurs (not to be confused with ties) in the tablature or standard notation are articulated with either a hammer-on, pull-off, or slide. Lower notes slurred to higher notes are played as hammer-ons; higher notes slurred to lower notes are played as pull-offs. While it's usually obvious that slurred notes are played as hammer-ons or pull-offs, an *H* or *P* is included above the tablature as an extra reminder.

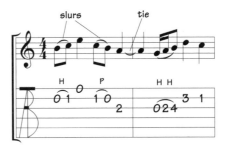

Slides are represented with a dash, and an *S* is included above the tab. A dash preceding a note represents a slide into the note from an indefinite point in the direction of the slide; a dash following a note indicates a slide off of the note to an indefinite point in the direction of the slide. For two slurred notes connected with a slide, you should pick the first note and then slide into the second.

Bends are represented with upward curves, as shown in the next example. Most bends have a specific destination pitch—the number above the bend symbol shows how much the bend raises the string's pitch: ¼ for a slight bend, ½ for a half step, 1 for a whole step.

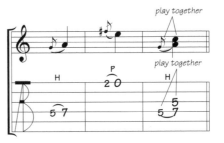

Grace notes are represented by small notes with a dash through the stem in standard notation and with small numbers in the tab. A grace note is a very quick ornament leading into a note, most commonly executed as a hammer-on, pull-off, or slide. In the first example below, pluck the note at the fifth fret on the beat, then quickly hammer onto the seventh fret. The second example is executed as a quick pull-off from the second fret to the open string. In the third example, both notes at the fifth fret are played simultaneously (even though it appears that the fifth fret, fourth string, is to be played by itself), then the seventh fret, fourth string, is quickly hammered.

HARMONICS

Harmonics are represented by diamond-shaped notes in the standard notation and a small dot next to the tablature numbers. Natural harmonics are indicated with the text "Harmonics" or "Harm." above the tablature. Harmonics articulated with the right hand (often called artificial harmonics) include the text "R.H. Harmonics" or "R.H. Harm." above the tab. Right-hand harmonics are executed by lightly touching the harmonic node (usually 12 frets above the open string or fretted note) with the right-hand index finger and plucking the string with the thumb or ring finger or pick. For extended phrases played with right-hand harmonics, the fretted notes are shown in the tab along with instructions to touch the harmonics 12 frets above the notes.

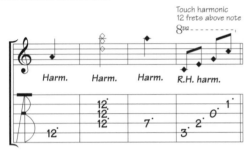

REPEATS

One of the most confusing parts of a musical score can be the navigation symbols, such as repeats, *D.S. al Coda, D.C. al Fine, To Coda*, etc. Repeat symbols are placed at the beginning and end of the passage to be repeated.

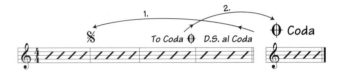

You should ignore repeat symbols with the dots on the right side the first time you encounter them; when you come to a repeat symbol with dots on the left side, jump back to the previous repeat symbol facing the opposite direction (if there is no previous symbol, go to the beginning of the piece). The next time you come to the repeat symbol, ignore it and keep going unless it includes instructions such as "Repeat three times."

A section will often have a different ending after each repeat. The example below includes a first and a second ending. Play until you hit the repeat symbol, jump back to the previous repeat symbol and play until you reach the bracketed first ending, skip the measures under the bracket and jump immediately to the second ending, and then continue.

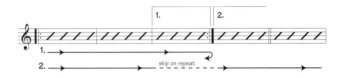

D.S. stands for *dal segno* or "from the sign." When you encounter this indication, jump immediately to the sign (𝄋). D.S. is usually accompanied by *al Fine* or *al Coda*. Fine indicates the end of a piece. *A coda* is a final passage near the end of a piece and is indicated with ⊕. *D.S. al Coda* simply tells you to jump back to the sign and continue on until you are instructed to jump to the coda, indicated with *To Coda* ⊕.

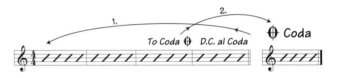

D.C. stands for *da capo* or "from the beginning." Jump to the top of the piece when you encounter this indication.

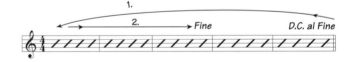

D.C. al Fine tells you to jump to the beginning of a tune and continue until you encounter the Fine indicating the end of the piece (ignore the *Fine* the first time through).

about the teachers

ANDREW DUBROCK

Andrew DuBrock grew up playing piano and horn and singing in choir. While pursuing a degree in music at Brown University, he decided it was finally time to pick up the guitar. In 1994, he began editing Hal Leonard's Signature Licks, Musicians' Institute, and Guitar School series. He also penned Acoustic Café, a monthly column in Cherry Lane's *Guitar One* magazine. He now translates outlandish tunings and bizarre techniques to paper as *Acoustic Guitar* magazine's music editor, and performs around the San Francisco area as a singer-songwriter.

MARK HANSON

A former editor at *Frets* magazine, Mark Hanson has authored more than two dozen instructional books and videos, many published by his company Accent On Music. As a guitar soloist, Hanson regularly travels the country, presenting concerts and guitar master classes. He has shared the stage with such luminaries as John Renbourn, the late Jerry Garcia, Laurence Juber, and Alex de Grassi. Hanson's music is heard regularly on syndicated TV and radio programs, and he has taught guitar at several institutions of higher learning, including Stanford University. Hanson lives near Portland, Oregon, and his Web site is www.accentonmusic.com.

GARY JOYNER

Gary Joyner teaches private students, clinics, and classes about acoustic guitar, fingerstyle guitar, guitar tunings, songwriting, music theory, performance, and creativity. He also works as a freelance writer, writing teacher and consultant, and librettist. He composes music and text for guitar, voice, electronic music recordings, and theater. He lives in St. Paul, Minnesota.

DALE MILLER

Dale Miller is a fingerstyle guitarist, guitar teacher, music store owner, freelance writer, and computer consultant living in Berkeley, California. His earliest guitar idol was John Fahey, and his first solo recording was *Fingerpicking Rags and Other Delights* (re-released by Fantasy Records in 1998). His most recent album, *Both of Me* (Dale Miller Productions), features duets of jazz standards played on a National steel and Martin wooden guitars. Miller is the author of two book/CD combos from Mel Bay Publications and is featured on two Mel Bay compilations as well as several other String Letter Publishing books. His Web site is dalemiller.com.

KEN PERLMAN

Ken Perlman is a five-string banjo player (and pioneer of the melodic clawhammer style) and fingerstyle guitarist who plays old-time blues, ragtime, and folk music, as well as Celtic and North American fiddle tunes. He is also an acclaimed music teacher who has released a variety of banjo and guitar instruction books and tapes for Mel Bay, Centerstream, and Homespun Tapes. Perlman spent more than a decade collecting tunes and oral histories from traditional fiddle players on Prince Edward Island in eastern Canada, published a book of these fiddle transcriptions, and produced field recordings on Rounder, Marimac, and Mel Bay.

AL PETTEWAY

Al Petteway is the coordinator for the Swannanoa Gathering's Guitar Week and teaches private lessons in his home in Takoma Park, Maryland. He has won more than three dozen awards from the Washington Area Music Association and the Maryland State Arts Council. *Racing Hearts*, his sixth recording and first entirely collaborative effort with his wife, Amy White, was released in February 2000 on the Fairewood label. They have also released a duo guitar recording for the Groovemasters series on Solid Air Records. Petteway can be reached on the Web at www.fairewood.com.

HAPPY TRAUM

During the past forty years, Happy Traum's avid interest in traditional and contemporary music has brought him recognition as a performer, writer, editor, folklorist, teacher, and recording artist. He has performed throughout the world and has appeared on recordings as a featured artist, as well as on sessions with Bob Dylan, Chris Smither, Maria Muldaur, Eric Andersen, Rory Block, Jerry Jeff Walker, Allen Ginsberg, and many others. Traum is the author of more than a dozen bestselling guitar instruction books and, as founder of Homespun Tapes, has produced more than 400 music lessons taught by top professional performing musicians on videos, CDs, and cassettes.

Building Fingerstyle Arrangements

Andrew DuBrock

Unless you're Mozart or Beethoven, you probably don't find complete symphonies floating around in your brain. But you might experience nifty single-note melodies that come to you while you're showering, doing the laundry, or perhaps eating a particularly tasty chocolate bar. Turning these melodies into complete fingerstyle guitar arrangements isn't as hard as it may seem, especially if you break down the process into several steps. In this lesson we'll look at how to build an arrangement of a melody from the ground up by working on the traditional tune "Greensleeves."

KNOW THE MELODY

Although you may be able to whistle the melody backward in your sleep, it's always good to determine where a tune lies on the fretboard so you don't plunge headfirst into a dead-end arrangement. Make sure you learn the piece with all the correct notes, because it is harder to unlearn a mistake than it is to learn the song correctly the first time. Example 1 shows the melody of "Greensleeves" in root position. Play it through several times before moving on to the next step.

Introduction **TRACK 2**

TRACK 3 Ex. 1 "Greensleeves" melody

HARMONIZE THE MELODY

Harmonize the melody is really just a fancy way of saying *add some chords to the melody*. You can harmonize your melody in many different ways. The simplest way is to look up the melody in a book and use the chords listed there! But I would recommend not relying on this crutch too often. Instead, try listening to recordings and using your ear to pick the chord progression out of the mix. This method gives you hands-on experience while developing your ear at the same time. A third way to harmonize your melody is to come up with your own chord progression. You can get started by checking out a book or listening to a recording and then adding twists of your own, or you can create the whole progression based on how you *want* the tune to sound. Remember that there is no "right way" to harmonize a progression; this is *your* arrangement. The chord diagrams in Example 2 show how I've harmonized the melody of "Greensleeves." Notice that some of the chords are unexpected (for example, the E-minor chord in measure 4 and the F-major-seventh chord in measure 6).

TRACK 4 Ex. 2 "Greensleeves" harmonized with bass line

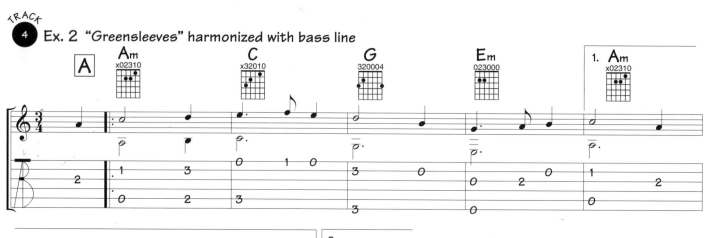

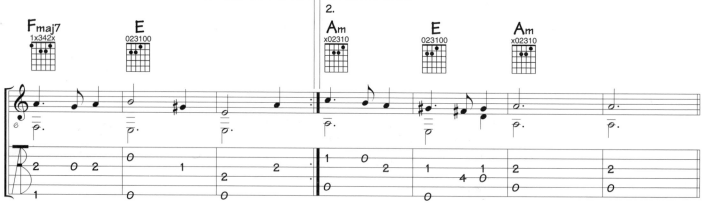

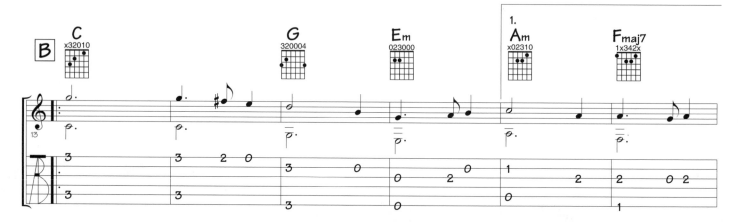

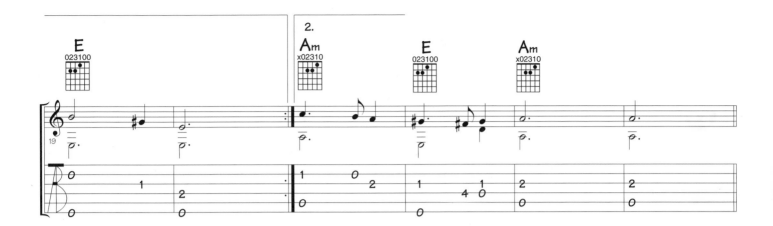

ADD A BASS LINE

After harmonizing the melody, you've essentially got a rough draft of your bass line. Just follow the lowest notes of each chord in the progression, and there it is! The down-stemmed notes in Example 2 show the basic bass line for my arrangement of "Greensleeves." But if you play Example 2, you'll notice that I haven't followed the chord progression exactly. In measure 1, I've added a walking bass line to join the A-minor chord to the C chord in the following measure. Walking bass lines generally move through adjacent notes from one chord tone to another, and they are a great way to connect bass notes in an arrangement. Also note that I've added a D bass note in measures 10 and 22, effectively changing the sound of the E chord to an E7 chord.

FILL OUT THE ARRANGEMENT

Here's where you get to stretch out a bit. One of the first things to consider when filling in an arrangement is the feel of the piece. Think about the song as a whole and how you want it to sound. Consistency is important; switching from solid 16th-note accompaniment to whole-note droning may sound a little forced. In the final arrangement, my goal was to fill out the piece with the modern-day melody but give it a more Elizabethan flavor; the rolled (quickly arpeggiated) chord on the downbeat of each measure helps bring this feeling across. The basic philosophy was to fill in the chords on the downbeat with these strums and then arpeggiate behind the melody throughout the rest of each measure. As a general rule, try using your thumb (p) on the lowest note of each chord and your index (i), middle (m), and ring (a) fingers to grab the rest of the chord. You'll need to move this formation around a little to get every chord, and you may find the E chord in measure 7 a bit tricky. You'll need to separate your ring finger from your middle finger by one string to get the B note on the downbeat of the measure.

Take into consideration the playability of your arrangement. You can invent the most amazing arrangement in the world, but what good is it if you can't play it? In my final arrangement, for instance, the pull-off in measure 2 is easier to perform than picking both notes would be, and picking the two-note chord at the beginning of measure 3 is a lot easier than strumming a whole chord right after your index finger hits the open G string on the *and* of beat 3 in the previous measure.

Once you've established some consistency in your arrangement, you can start exploring minor variations. For the second section of the piece (measures 13–25), I've varied the rhythm by shifting the two eighth notes from the first beat to the second beat in the first few measures. This subtle change keeps the song from sounding too much like a computerized arrangement.

Also check out the harmonic variation on the last note of the piece. That A major sounds great but also a little odd, since we've been in A minor. This substitution of the major third for the minor third at the end of a piece was common in late Renaissance and Baroque music—enough so that they came up with a special name for it: the Picardy Third.

Finally, break some rules! Following any formula precisely can create sterile-sounding arrangements. In measure 22, I've added a scalar run in the bass. This line is similar to the one in measure 9, but the extra few notes make it the most difficult measure in the piece. There are several ways to play this measure, but try out the suggested fingering first. If this ties your fingers in knots, you can always substitute measure 9 for measure 22 and come back to it once you've got it under control. I decided to break the rules again by changing the rhythm of the melody itself in measure 21 and adding an internal pedal point E to complement it. Deviating from the pattern can make a piece more interesting, but be careful not to overdo it. If every measure deviated, there would be nothing to hold the piece together!

USE YOUR EARS

Now that we've methodically built our arrangement, take a step back from the process and just play through the piece. Is there anything that you'd like to change to make it better? If so, *do it!* When it comes down to it, what really matters is that it sounds good, and all the analyzing in the world can't guarantee that your ears will be pleased.

Greensleeves

Traditional, arranged by Andrew DuBrock

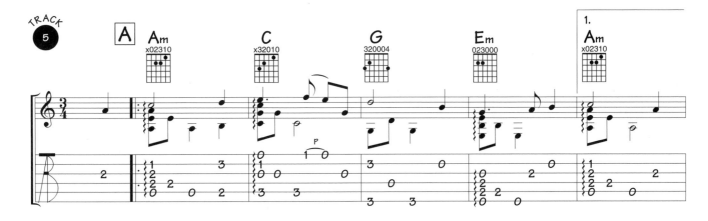

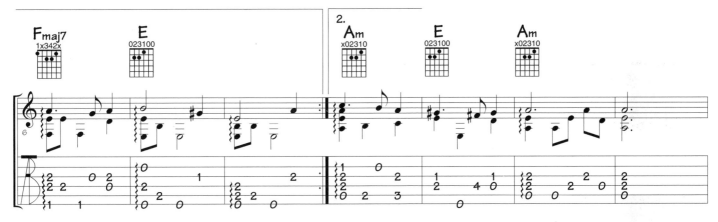

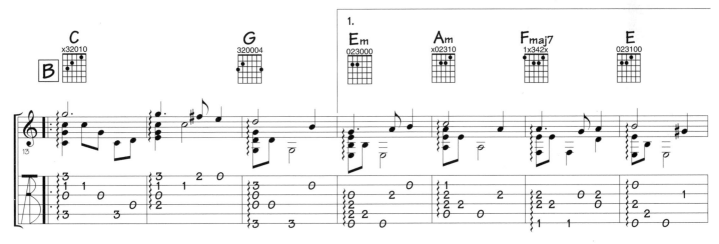

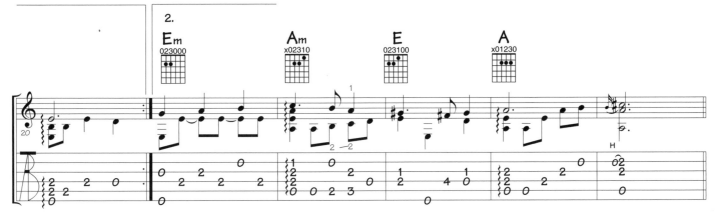

Alternating Bass Fingerpicking

Ken Perlman

Learning to set a melody over a bass line is the first step toward creating your own arrangements.

No matter how elaborate a fingerstyle arrangement gets, it ultimately boils down to playing a melody over a bass line. What's more, learning to set a simple melody over an equally simple bass line is the first step in developing the skills you need to create your own arrangements.

If you've done some fingerpicking, you are probably well acquainted with a technique called the alternating bass, which involves playing a bass string with your thumb on each and every beat of a tune in 4/4 time. To review the technique briefly: on the strong beats of the measure (beats 1 and 3), you play the lowest possible root of the chord (the note with the same letter name as the chord). On the offbeats of the measure (beats 2 and 4), you play another (or "alternate") bass string. So, on a C chord, for example, you'd pluck the fifth string fretted at the third fret on beats 1 and 3, and the fourth string fretted at the second fret on beats 2 and 4. I recommend that beginners use the fourth string as the alternate bass, except when the fourth string is already the lowest root note, as in a D chord. In that case, use the fifth string as the alternate. Example 1 lays out some alternating bass patterns for several chords.

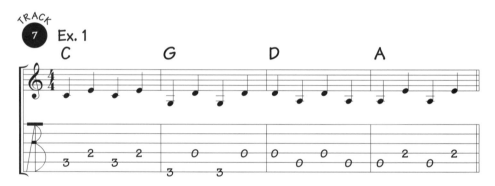

Since a major scale is just about the simplest and most straightforward "melody" around, you can master the rudiments of fingerstyle arranging by merely playing a simple major scale (or bits of that scale) over the alternating bass pattern for any major chord. Scale notes can be obtained in three ways. Some are already part of the chord form, some can be added to the chord form by reaching out with a left-hand finger, and some can be had by lifting up a finger from the chord to yield an open string.

Let's try some fingerpicking scale exercises, starting with a full G-major scale played on the treble strings over a G-chord alternating bass pattern:

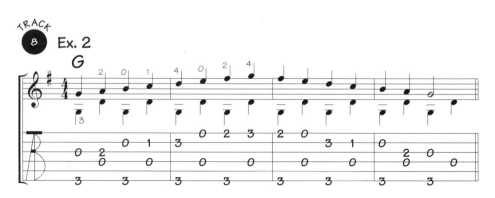

All the notes are sounded by pinching, or simultaneously playing, the bass note on one of the lower strings and the melody note on one of the top strings. For best results, follow the fingering suggestions in the music: the small numbers next to the notes on the music staff indicate which finger to fret with, where 1 is your index finger, 2 is your middle finger, 3 is your ring finger, and 4 is your pinky. I also recommend that you use your right-hand index finger to play notes on the third string, your middle finger to play notes on the second string, and your ring finger to play notes on the first string. Play through the scale/alternating bass combinations in the keys of C, D, and A (Examples 3–5) as well.

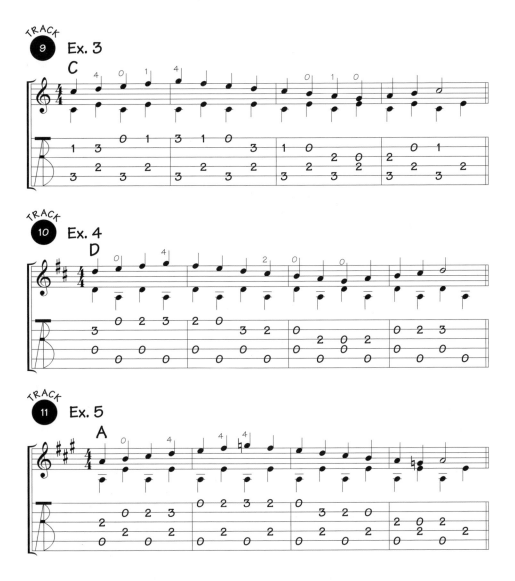

Once you're comfortable making your way through the scales, it's time to play a bona fide tune over an alternating bass. I've selected the common American song "Jesse James." Notice that each melody note is played as a pinch with an alternating bass note and that you fret the melody notes with the same fingers you used in the scale exercises. Observe also that long notes (half notes, dotted halves, and whole notes) are filled in by continuing the alternating bass pattern for the appropriate chord.

Try using this same approach to play some simple tunes you already know. Even if your first efforts involve songs no more complex than "Yankee Doodle" or "Twinkle, Twinkle," it will still be a major step forward. Don't choose a really complex piece like "Beaumont Rag" or "Mississippi Blues" for your first arrangement project or you'll be likely to encounter nothing but frustration.

Jesse James

Traditional, arranged by Ken Perlman

TRAVIS-STYLE ARRANGING

The drawback to simple alternating-bass fingerpicking is that it produces fairly boring music—the melody is just too regular. In general, no accomplished guitarist would create an arrangement for a tune that consisted entirely of pinches. To create interest, he or she would be sure to vary the location of melody notes relative to the various bass notes. In other words, some melody notes would be played as pinches with bass notes, while other melody notes would be played between the bass notes. In Example 6, all the melody notes are played between the bass notes.

Most proficient guitarists have an instinct for when to play notes as pinches and when to push or pull the beat. Although this instinct generally takes years to develop, there are formulas that allow even inexperienced players to get a feel for this more advanced approach to melody.

One simple path to advanced melody arranging is provided by adapting our original fingerpicking pattern to an alternating-bass style of guitar accompaniment called Travis picking. In its most basic form, Travis picking is a strict alternation of thumb-plucked bass strings and finger-plucked treble strings in the right hand while the left hand frets complete chords. All the treble notes are played in between the bass notes.

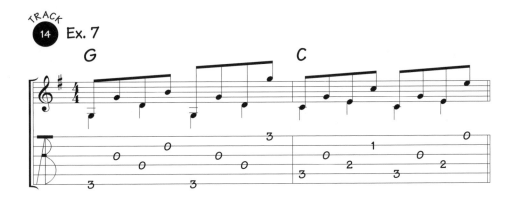

Example 8 shows a slight variation on this basic form. Play the first of the three melody notes in each measure as a pinch with the first bass note in the measure. Play the second and third melody notes in between the measure's other bass notes. Rhythmically, you've got a quarter note, four eighth notes, and a quarter note, counted *1 2-and 3-and 4.* This particular picking pattern is very satisfying rhythmically and makes for nice, sophisticated-sounding arrangements.

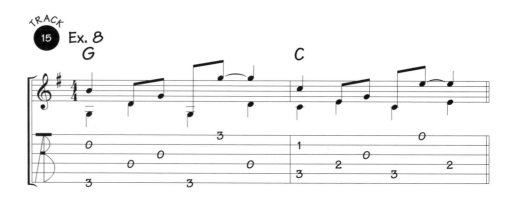

In Example 9 you'll find a scale that is organized in this kind of Travis-picking style. The first scale is in the key of G. Pinch the sixth string at the third fret (G) and the open G string (the third string) simultaneously and let them ring for a full beat. Then use your thumb to play the open D (the fourth string); your index finger to pluck the third string, second fret (A); your thumb on the low G; and your middle finger on the open B string (the second string). Finally, play the open D with your thumb once more and allow it to ring for another full beat.

Use a similar picking pattern (pinch, thumb, middle finger, thumb, ring finger, thumb) to play the scales in C, D, and A (Examples 10–12).

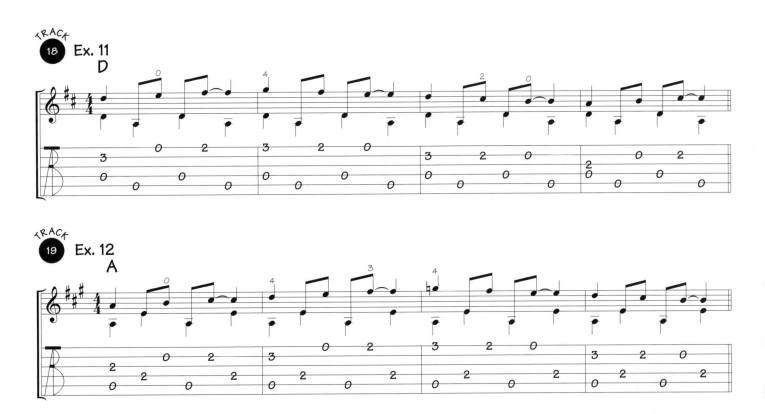

Let's try another arrangement of "Jesse James" (on page 22), this time focusing on this Travis-picking technique. Note that it sounds quite a bit spicier than the arrangement we looked at earlier. Use the same approach to adapt other melodies you're familiar with. Lots of luck!

Jesse James

Traditional, arranged by Ken Perlman

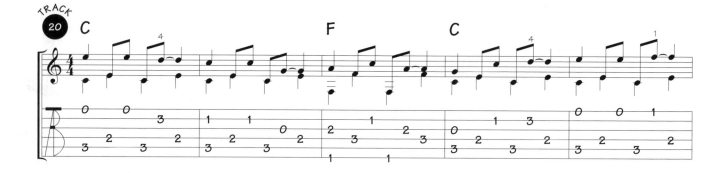

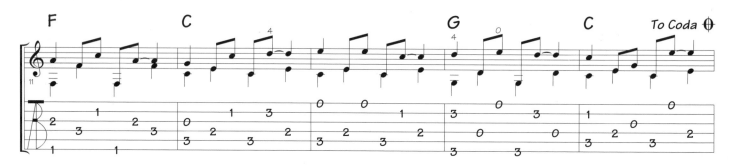

Playing Country Blues

Dale Miller

Learning to play fingerstyle blues can be rewarding for many types of players. With its simple chord shapes and steady rhythm, blues can provide the perfect way to improve your right-hand coordination and your ability to improvise in a fingerstyle context. There are many approaches to playing country blues; I've had the most success and enjoyment over the years with a style favored by Mance Lipscomb, Big Bill Broonzy, and Blind Boy Fuller, in which you keep a steady, thumping bass going with your right-hand thumb while playing melody notes with your right-hand fingers. This is similar to the alternating-bass style played so well by Merle Travis and Chet Atkins but has a darker, funkier, and muddier feel.

Begin by checking out these three easy-to-play first-position chords in the key of A.

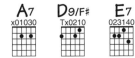

Finger the A7 chord and thump your right-hand thumb on the A (fifth) string in a steady 4/4 rhythm. As you get comfortable, work on making the sound funkier and darker by lightly touching the string with the meat at the base of your right-hand thumb. You can also experiment with hitting the bass string hard enough to sound out the next highest (D) string. Try the same for the D9/F♯ and E7 chords with your thumb moving to hit the lowest two strings. Now try the thumb technique through this basic blues chord progression at a slow, steady tempo. If you want to sing, do so as soon as you feel comfortable enough (I've added some words to show how they fit within the music).

Introduction TRACK 21

TRACK 22 **Ex. 1**

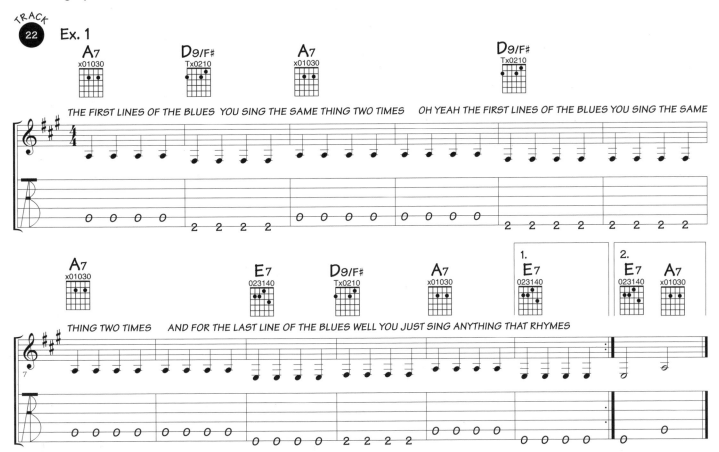

Next, let's add a simple picking pattern. As you can see in Example 2, some of the fingerpicked notes fall on the beat and some fall in between. Make sure your thumb continues to play on the beat no matter what your other fingers are doing. Tapping your foot can help. I've inserted right-hand fingering suggestions for using three fingers in addition to the thumb (*i* is the index finger, *m* the middle, and *a* the ring). You could also do the exercises using only the index and middle fingers. Just make sure to alternate the right-hand fingers when playing streams of eighth notes. This is an important habit to develop for fast, smooth playing.

TRACK 23 Ex. 2

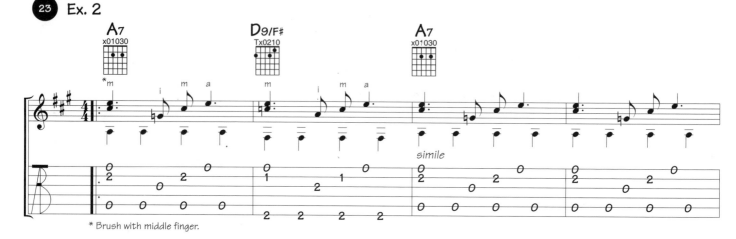

* Brush with middle finger.

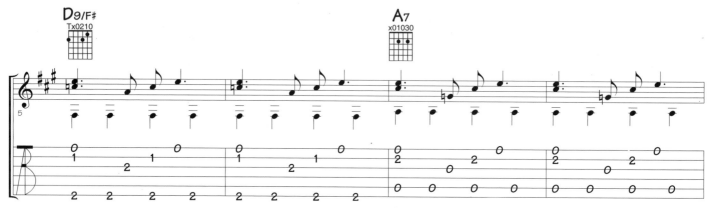

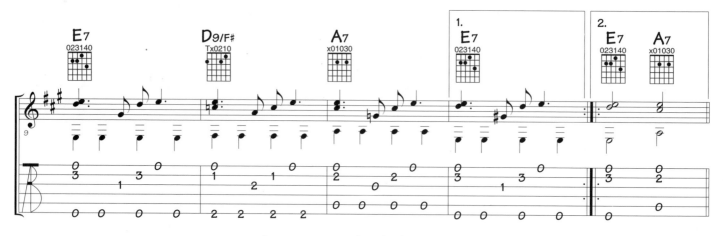

As you get more relaxed, add a new note to the A7 chord halfway through the first and fourth measures to double the G♮ note.

A7
x01034

As soon as you feel relatively comfortable with the first pattern, check out this second pattern:

Now play through the progression, alternating the two patterns.

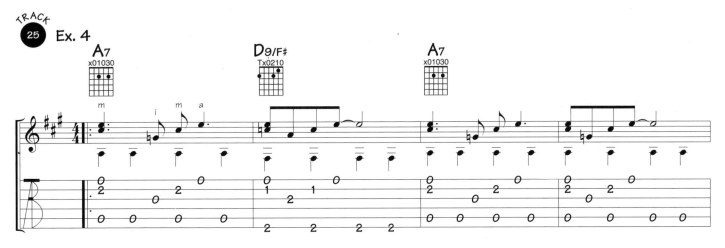

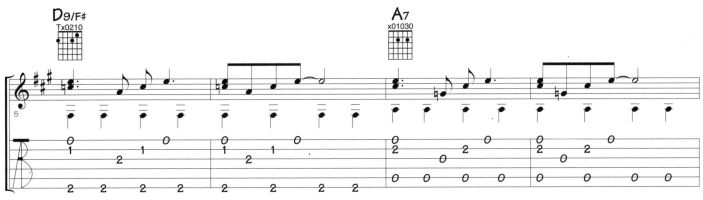

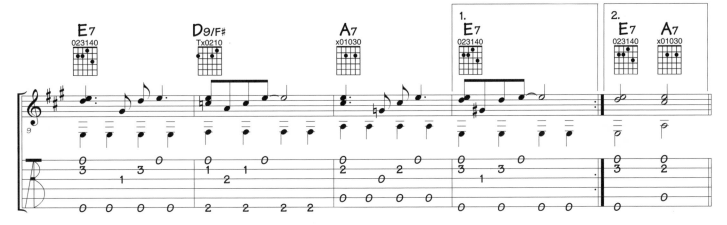

Begin to alter some of your left-hand fingerings by sneaking in a couple of easy-to-finger A7 chords, which you can substitute into any A7 measure.

When playing the chord up at the eighth and ninth frets (which you probably recognize as a D7 chord form moved up the neck), be careful to keep the open fourth string from ringing out. Either confine your thumping to the fifth string or mute the bass notes sufficiently so that they make an atonal thumping sound.

Becoming too enamored with pattern picking can paint you into a corner. Learning patterns is a good shortcut, but you should break out of the habit as soon as possible. Try this test. As you play Example 4, leave out the notes played by your fingers while you keep your thumb going. The sound of the thumb should be identical with or without the other fingers. If you can do this smoothly, you're in great shape.

In any event, let's break out of the pattern approach. Try Example 5 for the D9/F♯ chord. Play it for a moment as an isolated exercise, and then add it to the progression for one or more of the D9/F♯ measures. Blues licks in E often make use of a hammer-on from the G♮ to the G♯. Try Example 6 as a substitute for the ninth measure.

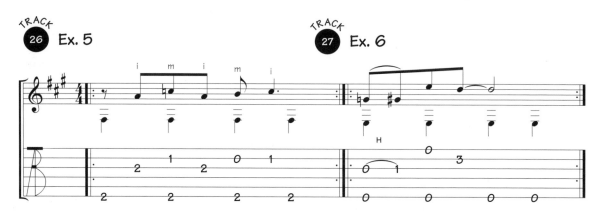

For the next addition, let's add a turnaround, a lick that occurs in the last two measures of the blues to bring things back to the beginning. Here is one in A used by the great Robert Johnson:

It is easier to sound the G♮ note by hitting the open third string, and you can play it that way at first. But playing the note on the fourth string produces a nicer descending sound and lets you add other techniques, such as snapping the string down on the fretboard. Be careful not to sound the open second and third strings. For much of the turnaround, notice how the index and middle fingers of the right hand alternate on the first string while the left-hand pinky stays anchored. Also notice how the change to the E7 chord occurs on the second beat of the measure with a hammer-on.

Here is a final version of our 12-bar blues using all the techniques you've just learned.

Dale's Blues
Music by Dale Miller

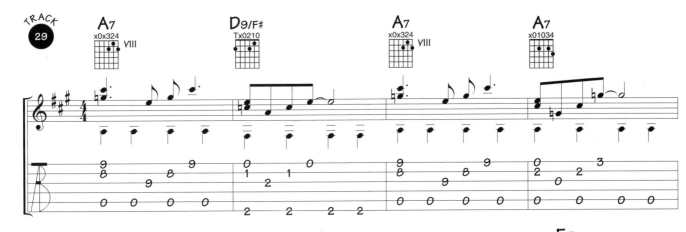

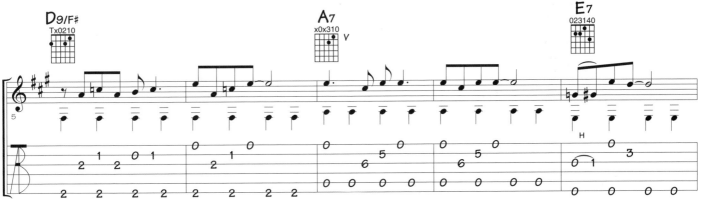

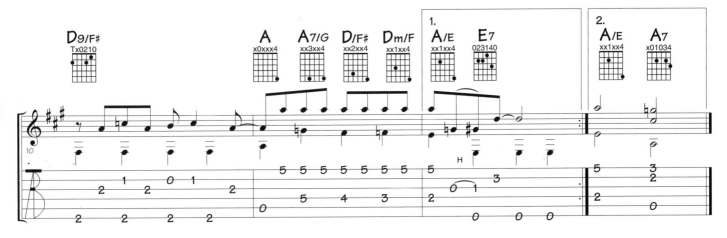

Hammer-ons and Pull-offs

Ken Perlman

Hammer-ons and pull-offs are two essential techniques that bring the notes to life.

Introduction 

Hammer-ons and pull-offs are two techniques guitarists use to produce notes with the fretting hand that increase the richness and expressiveness of their music. In the classical guitar world, both techniques are lumped together under the heading *slurs*. Example 1 shows how hammer-ons and pull-offs are indicated in notation: plucked notes are connected by arcs, or slurs, to neighboring notes. This notation tells you that one of the notes is obtained by the plucking hand and one by a subsequent action of the fretting hand.

Ex. 1

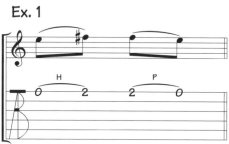

The terms *hammer-on* and *pull-off* were coined by Pete Seeger in the 1940s, when he was putting together *How to Play the Five-String Banjo,* which is now regarded as the first modern-style folk music instruction book. Seeger decided to present many of his arrangements in tablature—an age-old system of notation for fretted instruments that had been moribund for a couple of hundred years. As he was perfecting his own tablature system, he differentiated slurs into two distinct types. To reflect the specific movements involved, he called one technique a *hammer-on* and the other a *pull-off.* The names stuck.

THE HAMMER-ON

To perform a hammer-on, simply strike a sounding string with a fretting-hand finger, thus producing a new note. To indicate a hammer-on, the letter *H* appears in the tablature above the slur sign. Try a few hammer-ons that begin on open strings:

Ex. 2

For the first hammer-on in Example 2, pluck the open first string (high E) and then strike sharply down on that string with the middle finger at the second fret to get the F♯. Note that the transition from E to F♯ sounds much smoother when produced by a hammer-on than when both notes are plucked by the right hand. In the next hammer-on, pluck the open second string (B) and then strike sharply on that string with the index finger at the first fret to sound the C note. Work your way across the strings, making a smooth transition between the plucked note and the hammer-on each time.

To produce good hammer-ons, your fretting-hand finger must strike the string with concentrated force (imagine driving the string into the neck with a small hammer). To achieve that force, you need a little bit of elevation. In other words, the hammering finger must cock itself back ever so slightly before beginning its descent. Make sure that when you cock your finger back you maintain its arch, keeping both of your knuckle joints bent throughout the movement.

THE PULL-OFF

The second way to create a note with the fretting hand, a pull-off, is indicated in the tablature with the letter *P* above the slur (again, refer to Example 1). Start by plucking a fretted string. Then draw that fretting finger off the string in such a way that, in effect, it plucks the string again. To help you picture this process, observe that a finger is generally arched (bent at both joints) when it stops a string at a particular fret. To perform a pull-off, the inside of the fingertip is drawn in toward the palm. This movement compresses the arch of the finger, causing the fingertip to pluck the string.

Here are a few pull-off pitfalls to beware of:

• Keep your fretting hand still and draw your finger in toward the palm. If you keep your finger still and move your hand, you'll be way out of position to fret the next note.

• Make sure to keep your finger arched throughout the pull-off, so that you actually catch the string with your fingertip as you draw it inward. If you perform pull-offs by merely lifting your finger off the string, you won't get sufficient volume.

• Don't try to perform a pull-off by pushing your fingertip *away* from your palm. This technique can work on a limited basis, but it does not offer the strength and control of the pulling-inward method. Try these pull-offs:

TRACK
32 **Ex. 3**

To play the first one, strike the first string at the second fret to sound the F♯. Then, half a beat later, pull off at the second fret, yielding the open first string (E). Note that the transition from F♯ to E sounds much smoother when produced by a pull-off than when both notes are plucked by the right hand. In the next pull-off, pluck the second string at the first fret to get the C and then pull off to sound the open second string (B). Try playing pull-offs on each string as shown. When pulling off any string other than the first, you'll need to be careful not to let your fingertip collide with adjacent strings.

SLURS ON FRETTED STRINGS

Examples 4 and 5 show how hammer-ons and pull-offs can be performed on fretted strings. To hammer onto an already fretted string, keep the plucked fretted note sounding with one left-hand finger, then strike the string at a higher fret with another left-hand finger. If you need to stretch your finger out to reach the higher fret, make sure to do so *before* you start your hammering motion.

TRACK 33 Ex. 4   **TRACK 34** Ex. 5

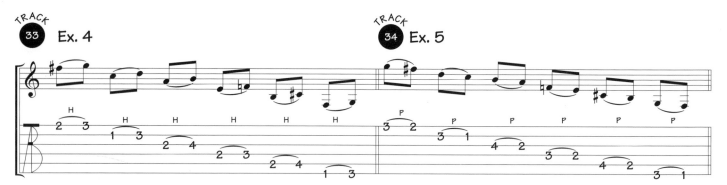

When performing a pull-off on a fretted string, start by fretting the plucked note and the slurred note simultaneously. Then peel away the higher finger, allowing the note stopped lower on the string to sound. To execute the first pull-off in Example 5, for instance, finger the first string at the second fret with your index finger and at the third fret with your middle finger. When you pluck the string, you'll hear the G note. Then, after half a beat has elapsed, peel away the higher finger from the G and allow the F♯ to sound. Make sure the F♯ is stopped very firmly at the second fret.

Example 6 shows some of the many combinations of hammer-ons and pull-offs that you're likely to encounter. As you practice them, remember the following rules. When executing multiple hammer-ons (Examples 6a and 6b), stretch the finger first and then hammer it down. Keep each plucked note firmly pressed down until the next hammered note begins to sound. When moving from a hammer-on to a pull-off (Example 6c), make sure to keep the hammered note ringing until you start your pull-off. When moving from a pull-off to a hammer-on (Example 6d), keep the slurred note ringing until the hammered note begins to sound. When playing multiple pull-offs (Examples 6e and 6f), fret all the notes at once and then pull off one finger at a time, keeping the others firmly pressed down.

TRACK 35 Ex. 6

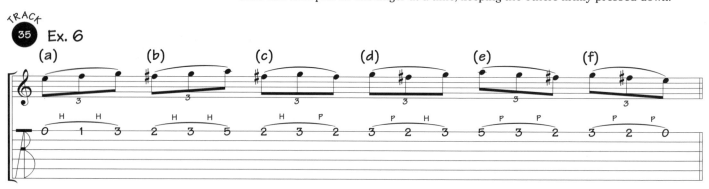

Practice these basic hammer-ons and pull-offs until they feel natural. Also try your hand at "The White Cockade," which was originally a Scottish marching song dating from the Jacobite Rebellion in the 1740s. It is still widely played as a dance tune in Scotland and the Canadian Maritimes.

The White Cockade

Traditional, arranged by Ken Perlman

USING THE TECHNIQUES

Now that you have a basic idea of how hammer-ons and pull-offs are accomplished, let's learn to incorporate them into fingerpicking patterns. In guitar arrangements, hammer-ons and pull-offs perform two functions. They can be used as embellishments or ornaments, and they can provide smooth transitions between melody notes.

Hammer-ons and pull-offs can embellish the music in two basic ways. First, long melody notes (whole notes, dotted halves, etc.) in arrangements can be filled in with hammer-on and pull-off patterns. Let's say you had a whole measure to fill in against an A-minor harmony. You could fill this in with the basic picking pattern shown in Example 7a. This pattern can be enhanced by substituting a hammer-on or pull-off for the first note (Examples 7b and 7c).

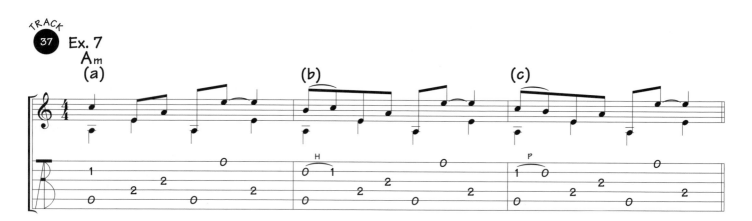

Moving this into the bass, let's look at a fingerpicking pattern on a G chord (Example 8a). Again, this pattern can be souped up by substituting a hammer-on or pull-off (Examples 8b and 8c).

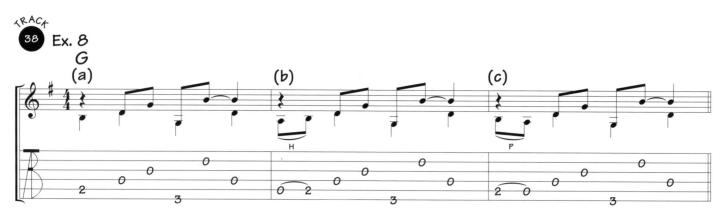

Second, any important melody note can be ornamented by turning it into a hammered note or a pulled note. Let's look at Example 7a again. Say we wanted to specifically ornament the C note (first fret, second string). We could turn the C into a hammer-on (Example 7b), or we could ornament the B note by turning it into a pull-off (Example 7c). In the Scottish tradition, this kind of ornamentation is called a slow grace note. In classical music, it's called an appoggiatura (a-pah-ja-TOO-ra).

SLURRING FOR SMOOTHNESS

No matter how accomplished a fingerpicker is, there is still a choppiness inherent in the technique of plucking successive notes on the same string. Hammer-ons and pull-offs, on the other hand, produce multiple notes with the same right-hand stroke and lend arrangements an extra degree of smoothness between notes.

Check out the simple slur exercises in the key of G presented in Example 9. To play these eighth-note scales, use a combination of plucked, hammered, and pulled notes. Make sure that each note gets the same time value (a half beat) regardless of how it's obtained.

Example 10 shows a modification of the exercise, where the hammer-ons and pull-offs are played over an alternating bass for the G chord. To make this work, you must hold your third finger down on the third fret of the sixth string (low G).

Another effective exercise is shown in Example 11. You obtain a series of triplets (three-note groups) through a combination of plucked, hammered, and pulled notes. I'll walk you through the first example. Pluck the open first string, hammer onto the second fret, and keep it ringing. Then (without allowing the ringing to cease), pull your finger off the second fret. Try this entire exercise on each string.

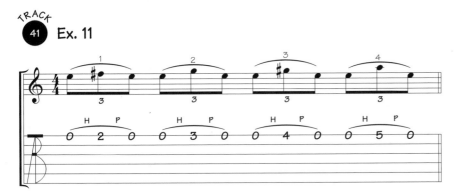

A more advanced form of this exercise is shown in Example 12, where hammered and pulled triplets are played over a fretted string. In the first triplet, stop the second fret of the first string with your first finger. Then, keeping the second fret firmly stopped, hammer onto the third fret with your second finger. Finally, use the second finger to pull off of the third fret. Again, try the entire exercise on each string.

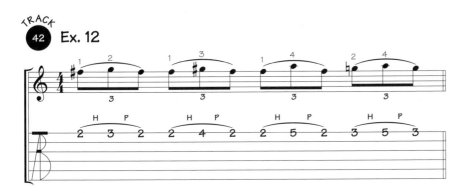

PHRASING

Phrasing is one of those subtle musical issues that separates accomplished players from hobbyists. In a nutshell, each melody is divided up into a number of submelodies or phrases. Each phrase ends on an ever-so-slight pause, and the next phrase begins with an ever-so-slight feeling of acceleration. Hammer-ons and pull-offs are excellent vehicles for bringing out the subtle phrasing of a guitar piece. When a series of relatively even notes is started with a hammer-on or pull-off, for example, the series tends to hang together as a single phrase, particularly if the series begins on a weak beat, or upbeat.

You can get the feel of a weak-beat hammer-on or pull-off by trying the picking patterns in Example 13. Note that the plucked note comes between the beats (that is, between two bass notes), and that the hammer-on or pull-off must be timed so that it falls in conjunction with the following bass note.

TRACK
43 Ex. 13

ADVANCED ORNAMENTATION

We touched briefly on multiple hammer-ons and pull-offs and hammer-pull combinations earlier in this lesson. These techniques are pivotal to playing ornaments and embellishments in a variety of genres.

You should be familiar with at least two such ornaments, decorative triplets and double grace notes, which are both offshoots of the hammer-pull triplets in Examples 5 and 6. Example 14 shows how a single note can be ornamented by transforming it into a decorative triplet or double grace note. Note that each ornament starts with a plucked note and is followed by a hammer-on or pull-off.

TRACK
44 Ex. 14

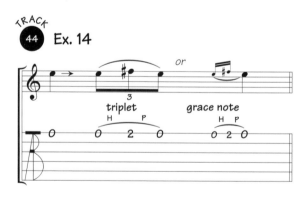

Now try your new skills in the traditional tune "In Old Colonial Days." I hope you enjoy it.

In Old Colonial Days

Traditional, arranged by Ken Perlman

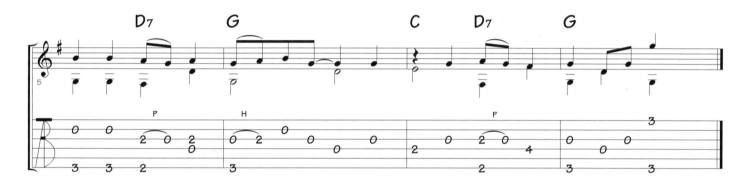

Dropped-D Tuning

Happy Traum

Only one note away from standard tuning, dropped D is a great place to begin your study of alternate tunings.

O f all the alternatives to standard tuning, my favorite is dropped D. Used by a host of professional acoustic guitarists, dropped D is also a good place for players unfamiliar with altered tunings to start. It's easy and quick to get into dropped D, it's extremely versatile, and there's a minimum of new fingerings to be learned.

To achieve dropped-D tuning, simply lower the bass E string down one whole tone to D, an octave below your open fourth string. It may take a little practice before you can retune your bass string quickly and accurately, but after a while the motion will become smooth. Check your tuned-down string against your open D on the fourth string to be sure it's in tune.

Now, with the lowered bass, you have a wonderfully rich D chord. Try playing these D-chord voicings, which include the basic position and two inversions up the neck.

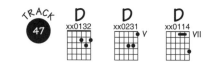

All those open strings give you a lush, ringing sound that you can't get in standard tuning.

Now that you've got the full D chord, you're going to have to adjust your other chord shapes to compensate for the lowered string; basically, you'll play the notes on the sixth string two frets higher than usual. Here are some of the chords you'll have to play in the key of D:

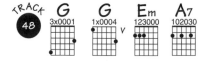

Dropped D gives fingerpickers a great deal of freedom in getting around the neck, since you don't have to worry too much about your bass notes. They just fall into place, particularly when you're on your tonic (D) chord.

"Worried Blues" is a perfect example of what you can do with this tuning. It's got only a few chord changes and can be kept quite simple, or it can be more complex, depending on your level of skill getting around the fingerboard. I learned it years ago from the singing of Hally Wood, a fine Texas folksinger. The melody appears above the arrangement.

Following the melody, you'll find two different guitar solos you can play to this song, one quite basic and the other a little more challenging. Note that I use the second-position D chord quite a bit. It gives me the melody notes I need and a good position from which to go up or down the fingerboard. See if you can make up some variations of your own. The version here was taken from my arrangement of the song on my CD *Buckets of Songs* (Shanachie).

Worried Blues

Traditional, arranged by Happy Traum

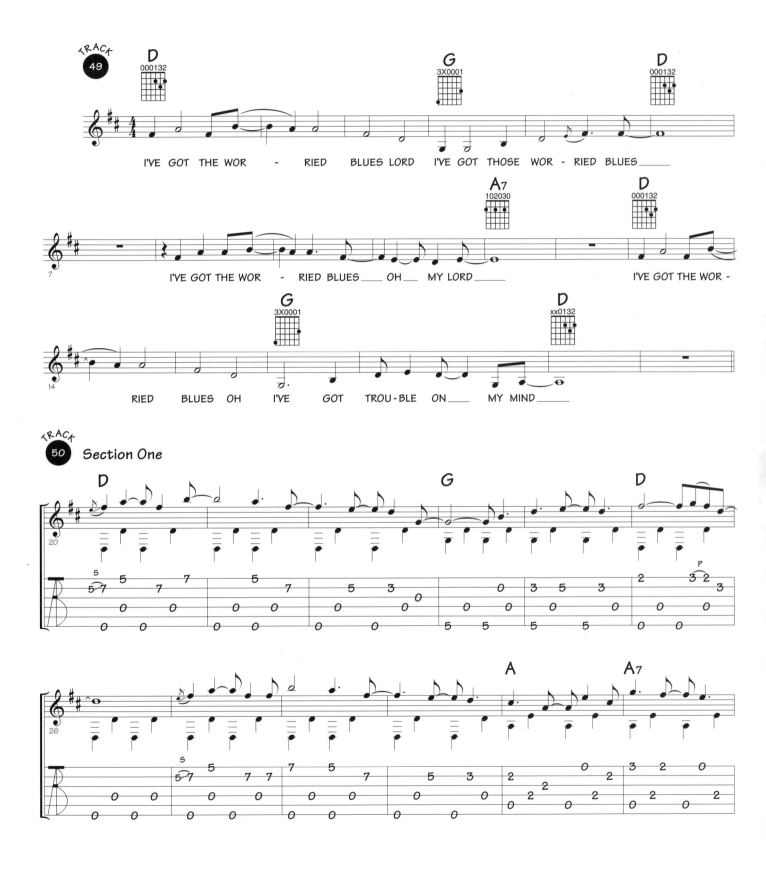

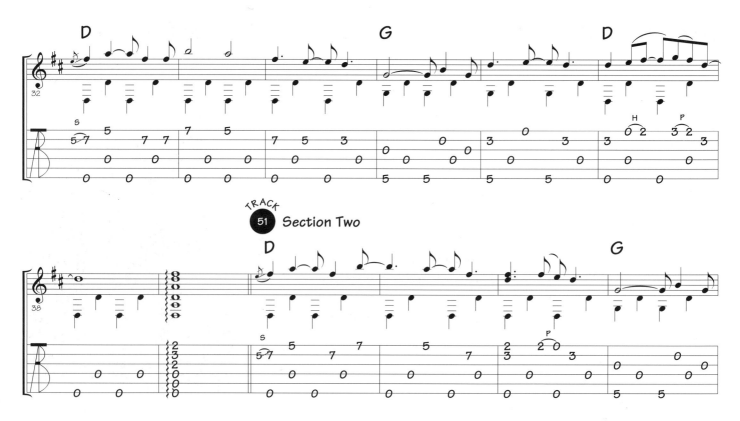

TRACK 51 Section Two

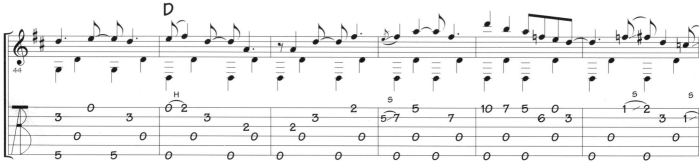

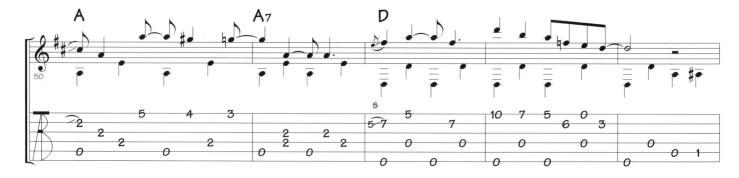

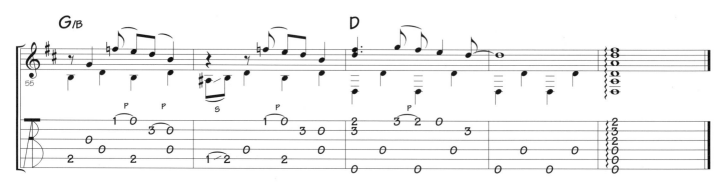

Celtic Songs in Standard Tuning

Al Petteway

So many guitarists play in open tunings these days that they sometimes forget about good old standard tuning—E A D G B E. Although D A D G A D or another open tuning may seem to be right for a traditional or Celtic tune, it's always worth checking out the possibilities in standard tuning. Recently, I decided to relearn all the Celtic tunes I had been playing in both standard and D A D G A D tunings. That way I wouldn't have to take precious time to tune during performances or travel with two instruments. I found that it was just as enjoyable to play the tunes in standard tuning as long as I found the right key positions. In this lesson we'll learn to arrange two Celtic favorites in standard tuning.

You can learn melodies by ear or, if you read music, you can find tunes in a Celtic music source book. Unfortunately the tunes in these books are not always written in the best key for creating solo guitar arrangements, so you must transpose them to keys that use open strings and allow you to play the entire melody without much difficulty. If the tune is in a minor key, you might try E minor, A minor, or D minor. If it's major, try G, C, or A. You can always use a capo to change the key, making it easier to back up a singer, play with other instrumentalists, or simply create a different quality for the piece. When I decided to arrange the Scottish favorite "Wild Mountain Thyme" I first tried the keys of C, G, and A. I soon discovered that G was the most compatible, since the entire melody falls under the fingers in first position.

I like to begin by playing the root note of the key under the entire melody somewhat like a bagpipe drone:

Introduction TRACK 52

You can even use this as part of the arrangement if it sounds good. In this case the root note is G. Listen carefully to the melody while playing the G drone in the bass. It sounds pretty good, but let's see if we can find some other chords to use.

In the key of G, the primary chords are G (I), C (IV), and D (V). Try the bass notes of these chords under different parts of the melody. Even though you are playing only the bass notes, place your fingers over the entire chord so the other notes of the chord will be available to you as you flesh out the arrangement.

TRACK 54 Ex. 2 Verse

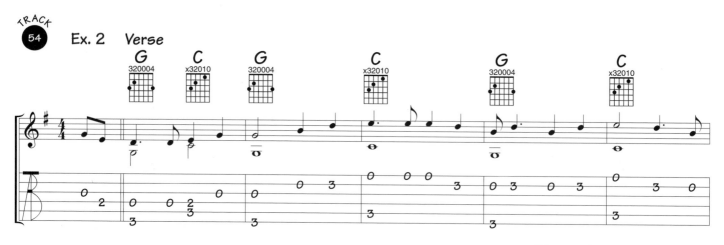

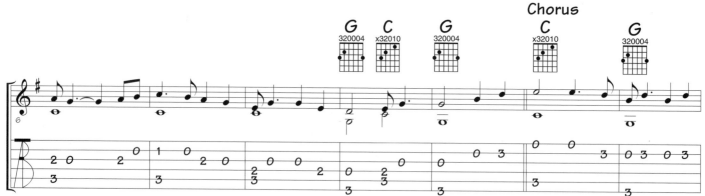

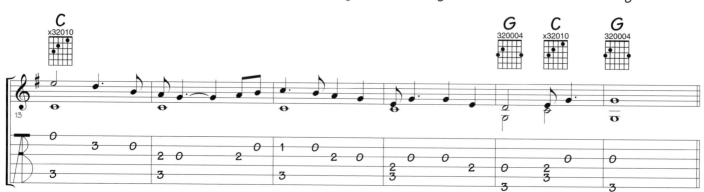

It seems as if G and C are the only two primary chords that work well with the melody in this case, so we'll need to get creative to make the arrangement more interesting. Example 3 shows you a few ideas. First, try using relative minors as occasional substitutes for the primary major chords. The relative minor is always found a minor third below the major chord. For example, you can try Em (vi) in place of G (I), or Am (ii) in place of C (IV). Another cool substitution can be found in the second half of the first section where the chord changes from A minor to F (measures 6 and 7). F is a major third below A minor, and though it is not the relative major of A minor, it's still a great substitution. Using the F chord gives you a little taste of the mixolydian mode, a very common Celtic mode based on a major scale with a flatted seventh.

You can also create more movement by using one of the other chord tones as part of a bass line. When moving from C back to G, for example, try using a B note in the bass to add a bit of motion against the static melody.

ARRANGING TIPS

Always play the melody notes the loudest, the bass notes a bit softer than the melody, and the chord fill notes a bit softer than the bass.

Relax the tempo slightly at the ends of phrases to make the music more lyrical.

Keep in mind the instrument(s) originally used to perform the piece. For "Sidh Beag, Sidh Mor," let the notes ring through whenever possible, especially in the bass. This technique will enhance the harplike effect.

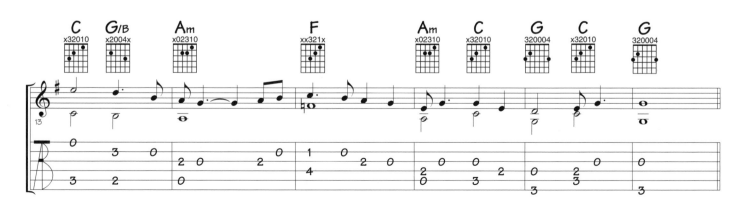

After the melody and accompanying bass notes and chords have been determined, you can begin filling in the chords and making the arrangement your own by adding ornaments, changing the phrasing, or doing anything else that seems appropriate. In this case, I've added extra measures after each melodic phrase to create a dramatic pause between lines. I borrowed this idea from a 1960s arrangement recorded by the Byrds that I really liked. I also decided to put the capo on the seventh fret to put me in the key of D and make the guitar sound more harplike.

Finally, I arpeggiated the chords by adding more strikes with the right hand fingers. It's best to start with the thumb when the arpeggio begins in the bass and follow through with the first, second, and third fingers in sequence. The left hand doesn't need to move to achieve this effect. Note that the direction of these arpeggios is dependent on the melody, so sometimes you'll find your right-hand fingers going the opposite direction—from the melody note rather than the bass. I also added a hammer-on/pull-off combination to the F chord during the chorus that leaves the open G ringing, creating a suspended second chord.

Wild Mountain Thyme

Traditional, arranged by Al Petteway

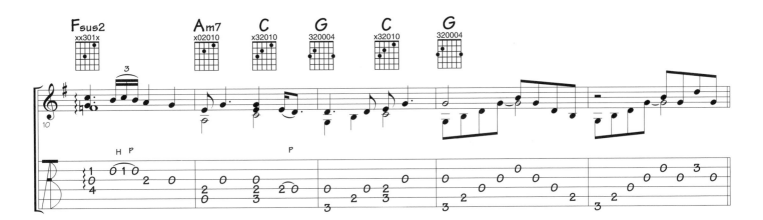

Chorus

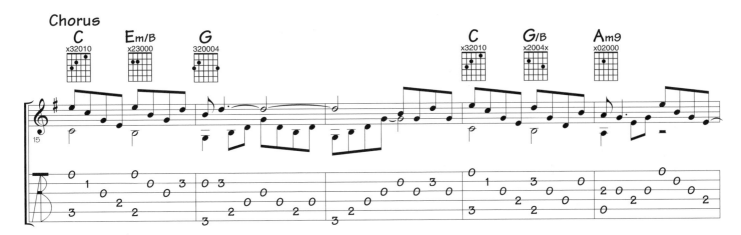

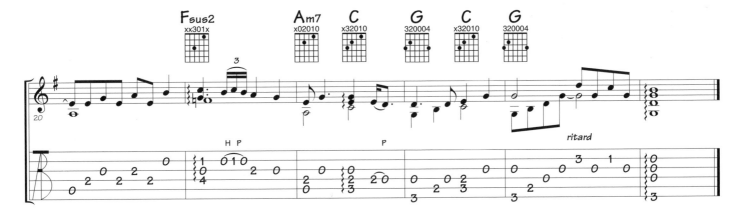

"Sidh Beag, Sidh Mor" is an 18th-century harp tune, written by the blind Irish harper Turlough O'Carolan, which has become a standard in the Celtic repertoire. After trying the tune in G, C, and D, I settled on C in standard tuning. In C position, most of the melody notes are reachable without leaving first position, and all the necessary bass notes are easily played. The third measure of the B section requires a position shift, but only momentarily. The rest of the tune returns to first position.

Since this tune is normally played in the key of D, put a capo on the second fret, making the root note of our C chord a D. Using the same methods as on "Wild Mountain Thyme," find the melody, then add the root in the bass as a drone.

TRACK 57 **Ex. 4**
Capo II **A**

B

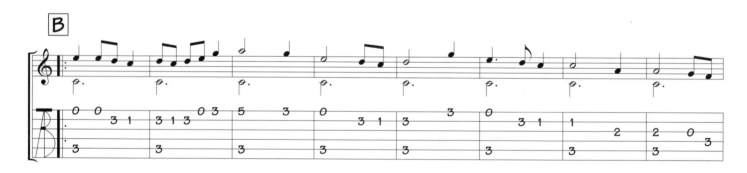

Once the basic location of the melody has been established, begin adding the most obvious bass note changes.

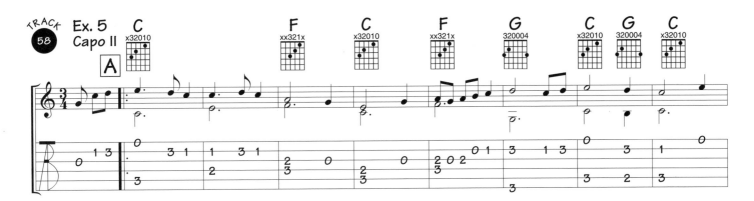

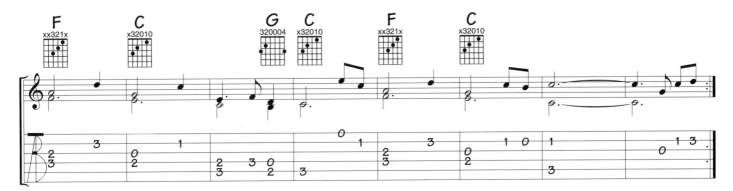

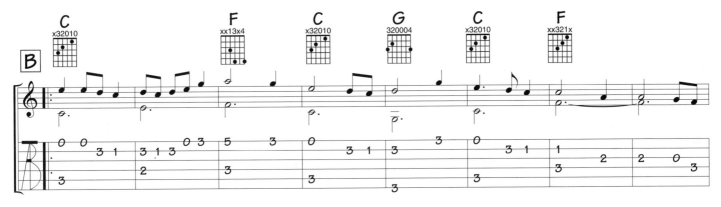

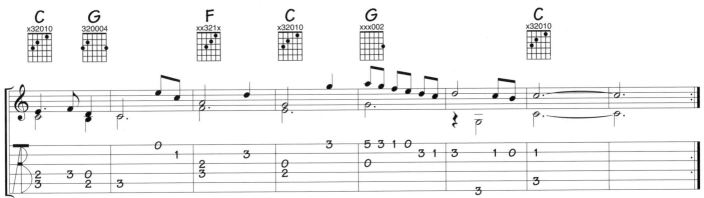

Fill in the chords and try using the relative minors as alternate chords. Then add ornamentation.

Remember that these examples are like road maps. They will get you where you want to go, but you must take your own scenic routes along the way if the trip is to be rewarding. Once you know the melody and chord structure of a tune, get away from the written page and work with the piece by ear. Not only will this give you more freedom to come up with original ideas, but it will also allow you to listen more carefully to the sound you are making and free you to play more musically.

Sidh Beag, Sidh Mor

Traditional, arranged by Al Petteway

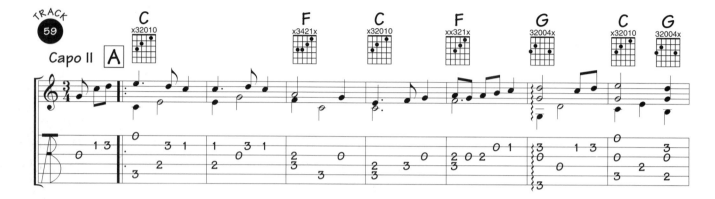

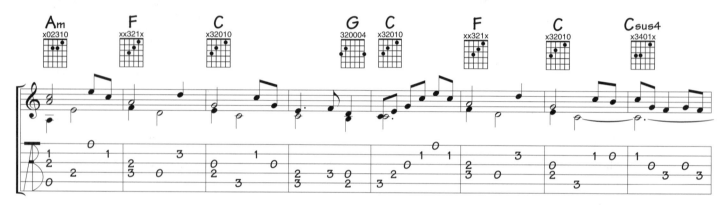

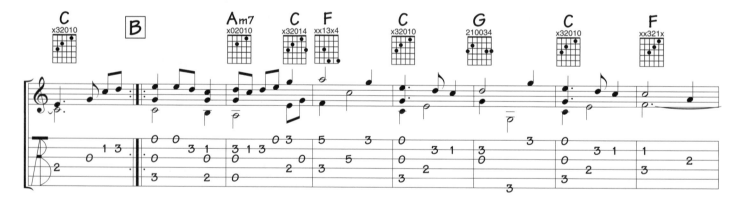

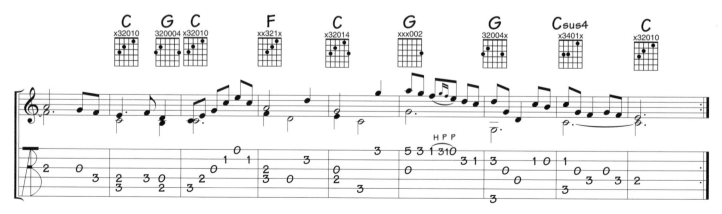

Hard Chords Made Easy

Mark Hanson

What do you do when you come across a B♭ or an E♭ chord in a songbook? Struggle with a barre fingering? Slap on a capo? Turn the page and go on to the next song? Take up the harmonica? All of these are possibilities, of course, but the idea is to play these chords, not succumb to them. You want to be able to make not-so-common chords sound good without hurting yourself in the process.

In this lesson we will dispense with barre chords, which are a handful for many guitarists. We'll learn some basic major and minor fingerings that will give you any major or minor chord you need, when moved up or down the neck, without pain and suffering!

Accomplished guitarists know that there are at least two possible fingerings for most chords. And almost every chord can be fretted in more than one position on the neck. The guitar is great in that way. What we are looking for are some of those alternative fingerings that will rid us of the "unplayable" chords. They do exist, and they are surprisingly easy to use.

MAJOR-CHORD FINGERINGS

Amazingly, a C-chord fingering is nearly all you are going to need to play any major chord you want to play. Try adding your little finger on the third fret of the first string of a normal, first-position C chord, like so:

C
x32014

Movable shapes can put intimidating chords at your fingertips.

Introduction
TRACK
60

I call this voicing of a C chord "Freight Train C," since almost everyone's version of that classic tune starts with this chord. It's a great voicing for a number of reasons. First of all, it's easy to play. Second, it has the root note in the bass—on the fifth string. Third, the four fretted strings provide all the notes of a major chord, and the fingering leaves a minimum of open strings to contend with. This is important as you start sliding fingerings up the neck:

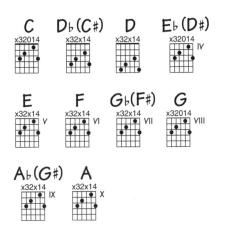

I use this fingering regularly (with my first finger on the fourth fret) to play an E♭ chord.

The only things to watch out for in "Freight Train C" are the two open strings: the third and the sixth. Generally, you can avoid picking the sixth string, unless your ring finger reaches out to fret it during an alternating-bass pattern (the tune "Tentacle Tango" on page 52 requires you to do this). You can pick the third string if it happens to belong to the chord, or you can avoid it by picking around it or muting it with the middle finger of your fretting hand. But with several of the chords, the open strings work beautifully as added color notes. On some of these chords you may lift your little finger and include the open first string:

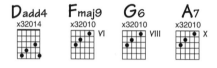

You may recognize the Dadd4 from "Kathy's Song" on the Simon and Garfunkel album *Sounds of Silence.*

The other major fingering we will use is F. Like most steel-string fingerpickers, I often fret the bass string with my thumb:

Finger this chord and slide it up the neck like this:

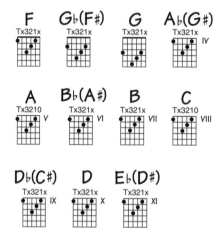

Watch out for the open first and fifth strings.

If you can't fret the sixth string with your thumb, play the F like this:

For these C and F fingerings, you will need to know the names of the notes on the fifth and sixth strings. When you use the C fingering, the note you are fretting on the fifth string tells you the name of the chord you are playing. For the F fingering, the root note of the chord is the note you are fretting on the sixth string. The chart on the right shows the names of these fifth- and sixth-string notes.

MINOR-CHORD FINGERINGS

Now let's look at a couple of easy and movable minor fingerings. The first one has its root note on the fifth string. The second chord's root note is on the sixth string. Start by fingering a first-position D chord. Move this one fret higher so that you are playing an E♭ chord. Continue to fret the two treble strings, but move your index finger from the third string to the fifth. Now the first, second, third, and fifth strings produce a beautiful, easy-to-play C-minor chord.

BASS NOTES UP THE NECK		
Fret	Sixth String	Fifth String
0	E	A
1	F	A♯/B♭
2	F♯/G♭	B
3	G	C
4	G♯/A♭	C♯/D♭
5	A	D
6	A♯/B♭	D♯/E♭
7	B	E
8	C	F
9	C♯/D♭	F♯/G♭
10	D	G
11	D♯/E♭	G♯/A♭
12	E	A

Cm
x1x032

We'll call this fingering the "spread D" chord. Here are the chords it makes as you move up the neck.

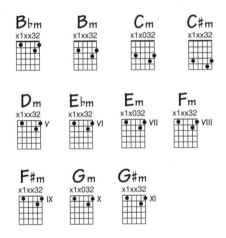

B♭m   Bm   Cm   C♯m
x1xx32   x1xx32   x1x032   x1xx32

Dm   E♭m   Em   Fm
x1xx32 V x1xx32 VI x1x032 VII x1xx32 VIII

F♯m   Gm   G♯m
x1xx32 IX x1x032 X x1xx32 XI

Check the chart and compare the positions you are playing with the names of the notes on the fifth string.

To use the next minor fingering, start by fretting the third fret of the sixth, third, and second strings as shown below. These three notes produce a G-minor chord at this position.

Gm
2x034x

In this position, you may play the open fourth string as well. Again, move this up and down the neck to see which open strings are harmonious with the fretted notes.

A variation on this fingering that I use continually is this minor-seventh fingering:

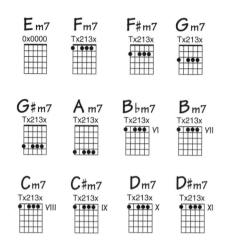

Usually I fret the bass string with my thumb, the fourth string with my middle finger, the third string with my index finger, and the second string with my ring finger. I use this fingering in an étude I composed in the key of E, which includes F#m7, G#m7, and C#m7 chords. If you play it correctly, it's a "Sweet Thing." Be aware that you can substitute the regular minor fingering for the minor sevenths in this tune. Simply pick the second, third, and sixth strings and you'll be playing a minor chord instead of a minor seventh.

With all of these major and minor fingerings, it is safe to pick the fretted strings no matter where you are on the neck. The open strings, on the other hand, may or may not work. Experiment to see which open strings are harmonious with which fretted positions. (If you study some music theory, you will learn which notes fit with which chords, so you can do this intellectually as well as aurally.)

There are many more relatively easy fingerings that I and thousands of other guitarists use in our playing, but what you have here will get you started. "Tentacle Tango" is a little fingerpicking piece in the key of E♭. Armed with what you have learned here, you should be able to play it. It uses both major and minor chord shapes, and the picking is a basic alternating-bass pattern. You might notice that this tune bears a passing resemblance to Ringo's "Octopus's Garden." Hence the title. Have fun with it and make sure you memorize the names of the chords as you play the tune.

Sweet Thing

Music by Mark Hanson

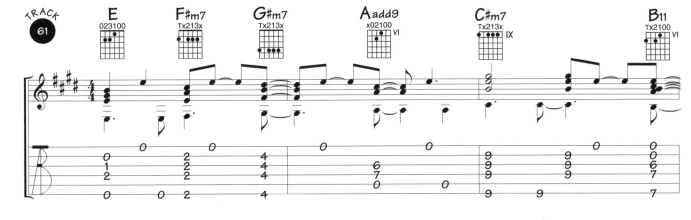

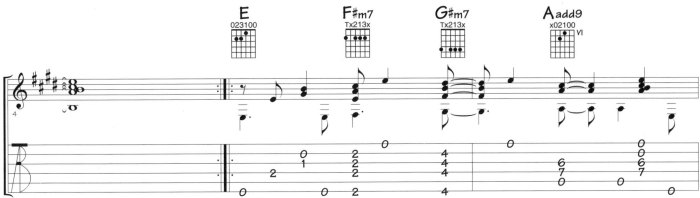

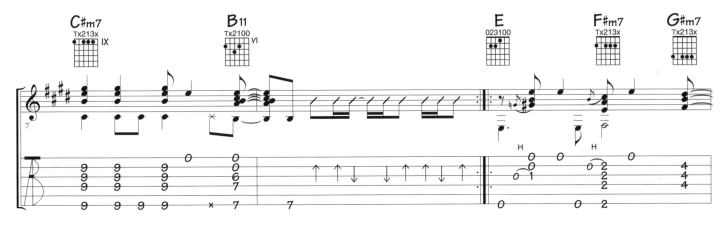

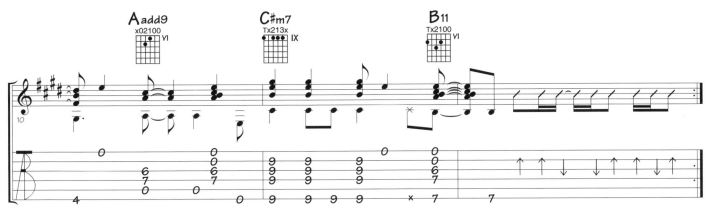

Tentacle Tango
Music by Mark Hanson

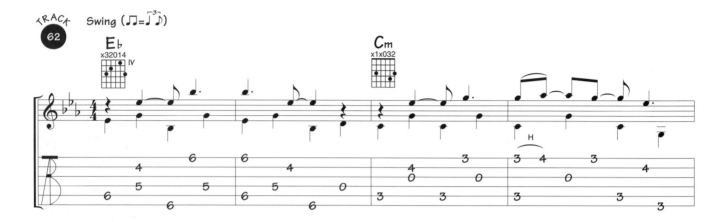

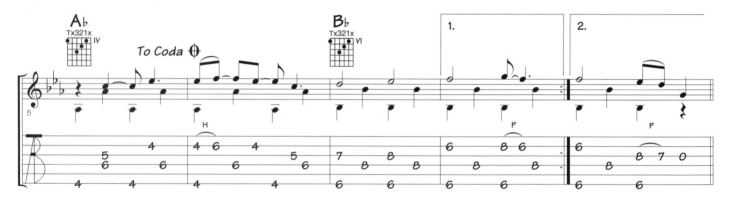

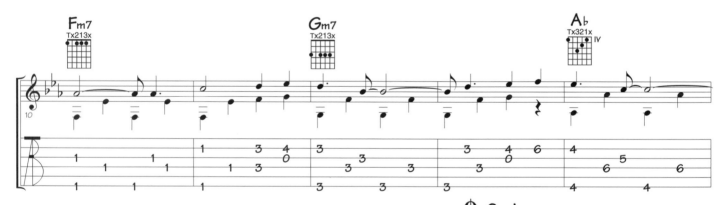

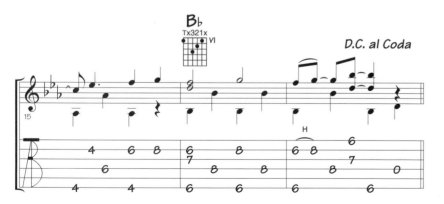

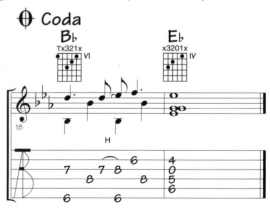

Great Classical Exercises

Gary Joyner

Elementary classical guitar exercises have much to offer contemporary finger-style guitarists. They provide an opportunity to practice reading standard notation, they're fun to play, and they're good for developing skills. You can use them to work on hand and finger independence, bass lines, intervals, voicings, and melodies.

As you begin the exercises, pay close attention to the fingering suggestions. You can try your own variations later. If you are a tablature reader, practice looking at the standard notation as much as you can. Tablature is great, but it's important that you learn to read music.

We'll start with some selections from Mauro Giuliani's popular *120 Daily Guitar Studies for the Right Hand.* This series uses the same C–G7 chord progression throughout the exercises. As you play through each measure, hold the entire chord down as you would when playing a contemporary folk-style pattern. Play the notes with downward-pointing stems with your right thumb.

In Example 1, your right-hand index and middle fingers pluck the first and second strings, while your thumb moves across the fifth, fourth, and third strings. Everything is played on the beat. Be sure to include the D note on the third fret of the second string in the G7 chord fingering. Work for a smooth right-hand motion and even tone and volume. As always, play slowly until you get it down.

Introduction

Classical exercises are a fun way to develop your fingerpicking skills.

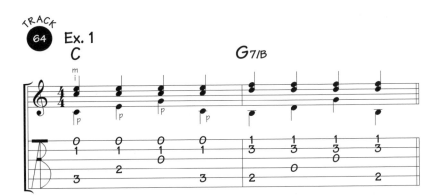

Examples 2 and 3 break the notes into triplet arpeggios. A handy way to count triplets is: 1-pa-let, 2-pa-let, 3-pa-let, 4-pa-let. This helps you keep your place in the measure as you count. Example 3 reverses the order of the index- and middle-finger notes.

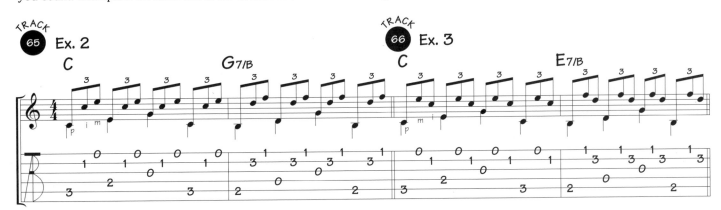

In Example 4 a right-hand pattern moves across sets of three strings at a time. This is a move that can be adapted as a flourish (for example, at the end of a verse or song).

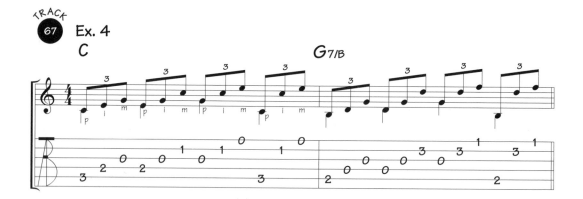

Ferdinando Carulli wrote many pieces to train the right hand. In Examples 5 and 6 we'll look at two typical Carulli arpeggio patterns that create a sustain effect when played quickly. It may take a couple of months of painstaking effort to make this work properly, so be patient. Take care to articulate the individual notes—it's easy to fall into a bass-and-block-chord sound, which isn't what we're after. Example 5 employs the triplet pattern with an alternating bass and additional chords.

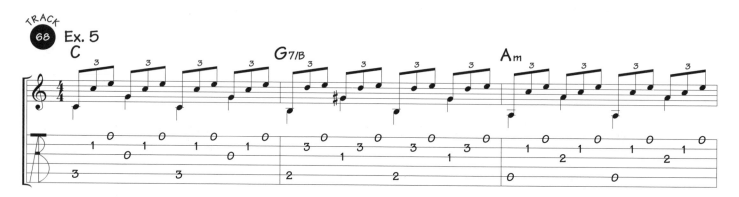

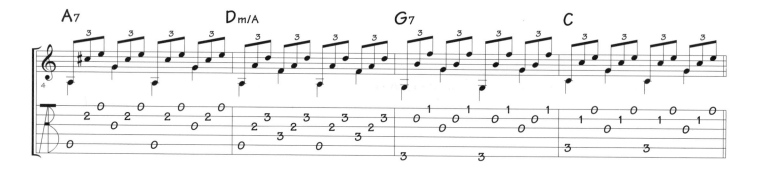

Example 6 is made up of 16th notes. Count 1-a-and-a, 2-a-and-a, etc., for this one. Notice the unchanging A bass note that functions as a pedal tone for much of the exercise. You might want to try muting that note with the heel of your right hand à la Mance Lipscomb.

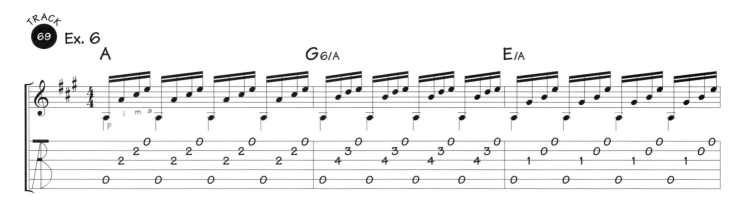

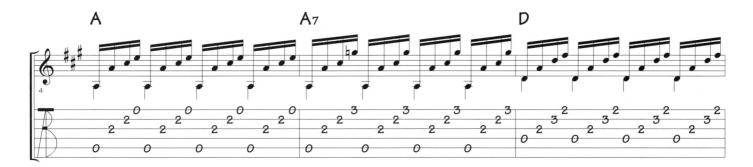

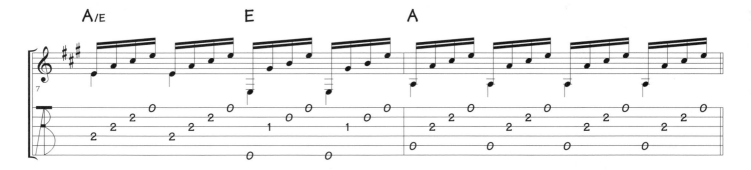

Henry Purcell's minuet (Example 7) gives you a chance to work on pull-offs—a technique that many of us tend to be sloppy with. Rather than play an anemic "lift-off," snap the string by pulling your finger into the neighboring higher string. Another useful tool, fretting with the thumb, has traditionally been avoided in the classical arena, but it's become an indispensable tool in contemporary guitar playing. Try it on the F bass note in measure 3.

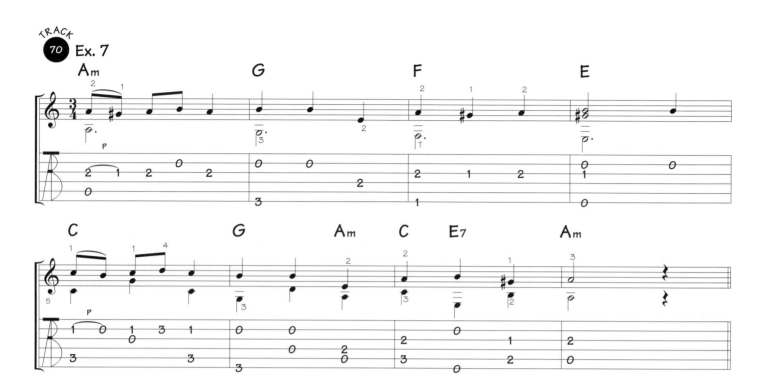

So far, our investigation of elementary classical guitar exercises has focused on arpeggio patterns. Now it's time to try some picking patterns that have scales woven into them. We'll also look at several studies that are actually small compositions.

Matteo Carcassi's method is a well-known tool for beginning classical guitarists. There are several editions of his work in print; my favorites are *The Carcassi Method* (Fischer) and *The Complete Carcassi Method* (Mel Bay). In Examples 8–10, you'll find some exercises combining a C-major scale with steadily repeated notes in another register. Example 8 places the scale in the bass region against a G on the first string. Carcassi's method suggests plucking all of the notes in the upper register with your middle finger.

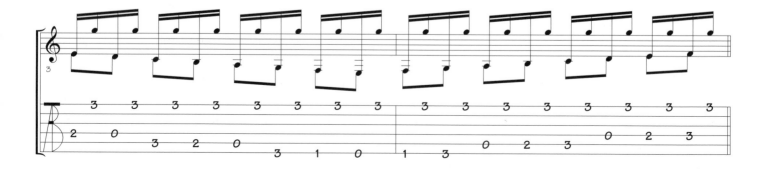

Example 9 moves the scale to the top strings, places the repeated G on the third string, and introduces an alternating bass line.

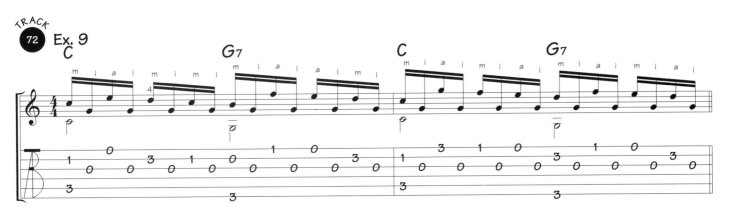

Example 10 is a hybrid of Examples 8 and 9.

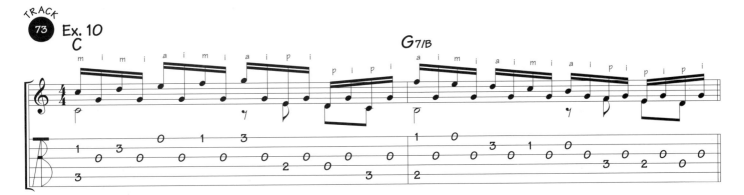

The trick with Example 11 from Dionisio Aguado is to play an unchanging right-hand *p-i-p-m* pattern (where *p* is your thumb, *i* is your index finger, and *m* is your middle finger) at all times. Your left hand will be busy in this first-position mini-workout, but it's quite playable.

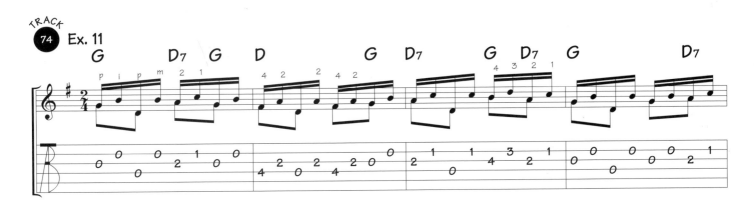

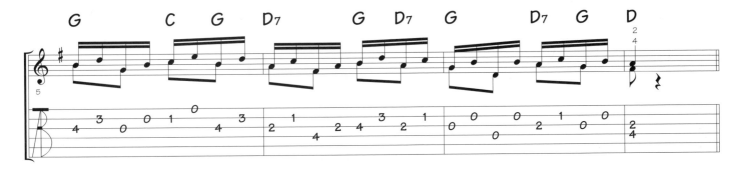

Example 12, another by Carcassi, also has plenty of action. On the first beat of measure 4, play a B and a C♯ on the fifth and second strings at the second fret. This may sound strange, especially after the preceding notes, but when you hear where the exercise is headed, it will make lovely musical sense. In general, it helps to remember that music usually moves forward toward resolution. If something doesn't seem to make sense, it usually helps to look ahead to see where it's going.

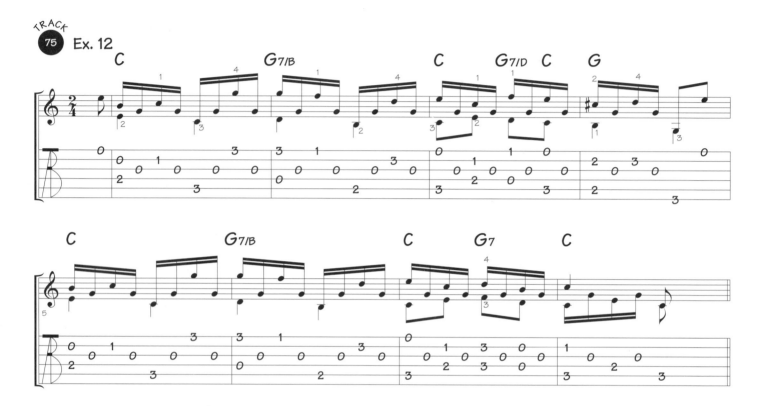

Carcassi's "Slow Waltz" is an easy yet evocative piece in A minor. The bass and treble runs, as well as the modulation to the key of C major, can be applied to contemporary works. The opening measures set up a rhythmic feel that will continue throughout the piece. Try hammering onto the C on the fifth string (third fret) or giving the E on the fourth string (second fret) a little juice with a light vibrato. The minor key of the opening section lends itself to expressiveness. Play around with the tempo to see how you can vary the effect.

Your right thumb will usually play three notes per bar. Watch the stems in the staff notation if you're confused about the fingering. The notes with the downward stems are played with the thumb unless otherwise noted. There are many options for alternate right-hand fingerings. Try as many as you can, and use that ring finger!

Here's one way to give the G♯ in measure 5 its full two beats: Finger it with your left index finger and roll the finger over to include the C on the second string while still holding the G♯ on the third string. Roll it back when you play the open second string. This rolling move is very useful for smooth phrasing in all styles. In measure 11, the piece shifts to the key of C, the relative major of A minor. Be sure to play this section at a steady tempo.

Slow Waltz

Music by Matteo Carcassi

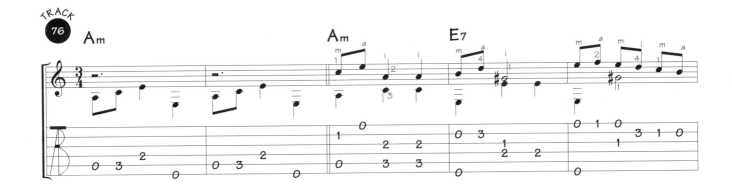

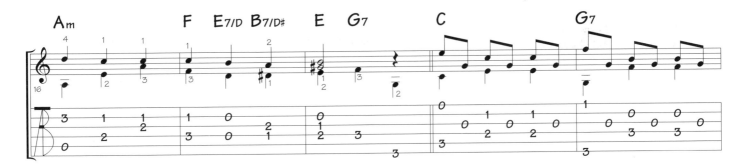

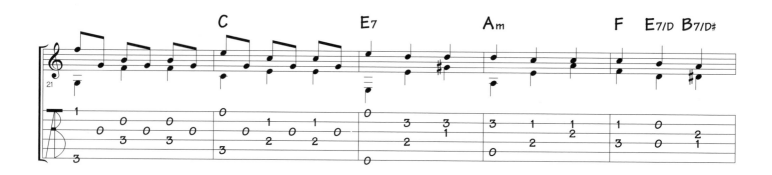

The E7 chord takes you back to the key of A minor in measure 16 and stays there until measure 18, when it steps into a suggestion of G7 that modulates back to C. Then the first C-major section repeats until measure 26, when a bass run leads once again to the theme in A minor. Try playing the bass run by alternating your right thumb and index finger. The same run closes the piece at the end of the repeated A-minor theme.

If this lesson has opened your ears to some new sounds and your fingers to some new techniques, it has done its job. And I hope that when you visit your local music store you remember to spend some time in the classical book bins on your way to the blues and folk sections.

Other Titles from String Letter Publishing

FLATPICKING GUITAR ESSENTIALS

Book and CD
96 pp., $19.95
Item #21699174
ISBN 1-890490-07-5

FINGERSTYLE GUITAR ESSENTIALS

Book and CD
96 pp., $19.95
Item #21699145
ISBN 1-890490-06-7

SWING GUITAR ESSENTIALS

Book and CD
80 pp., $19.95
Item #21699193
ISBN 1-890490-1

ROOTS AND BLUES FINGERSTYLE GUITAR

Book and CD
96 pp., $19.95
Item #21699214
ISBN 1-890490-14-8

ALTERNATE TUNINGS GUITAR ESSENTIALS

Book and CD
80 pp., $19.95
Item #21695557
ISBN 1-890490-24-5

ACOUSTIC BLUES GUITAR ESSENTIALS

Book and CD
80 pp., $19.95
Item #21699186
ISBN 1-890490-10-5

ACOUSTIC GUITAR LEAD AND MELODY BASICS

Book and CD
64 pp., $14.95
Item #21695492
ISBN 1-890490-19-9

SOLO FINGERSTYLE BASICS

Book and CD
64 pp., $14.95
Item #21695597
ISBN 1-890490-33-4

ACOUSTIC GUITAR ACCOMPANIMENT BASICS

Book and CD
64 pp., $14.95
Item #21695430
ISBN 1-890490-11-3

PERFORMING ACOUSTIC MUSIC

104 pp., $14.95
Item #21695512
ISBN 1-890490-22-9

SONGWRITING & THE GUITAR

96 pp., $14.95
Item #21330565
ISBN 1-890490-28-8

ACOUSTIC GUITAR OWNER'S MANUAL

112 pp., $17.95
Item #21330532
ISBN 1-890490-21-0

CUSTOM GUITARS

150 pp., $39.95
Item #21330564
ISBN 1-890490-29-6

CLASSICAL GUITAR ANSWER BOOK

84 pp. $14.95
Item #21330443
ISBN 1-890490-08-3

At your music or book store, or order direct • Call (800) 637-2852 • Fax (414) 774-3259 •
On-line www.acousticguitar.com

Also Available in the Acoustic Guitar CD Songbook Series

Each title has a CD with original artist recordings plus a book with complete guitar transcriptions. All include songs in both standard and alternate tunings.

FINGERSTYLE GUITAR MASTERPIECES

John Williams • Adrian Legg • Chris Proctor • Preston Reed • Ed Gerhard • Martin Simpson • John Renbourn • Leo Kottke • Jacques Stotzem • Peppino D'Agostino • Jorma Kaukonen • Duck Baker

72 pp., $16.95
Item #21699222
ISBN 1-890490-13-X

RHYTHMS OF THE ROAD

Bruce Cockburn • Toshi Reagon • Don Ross • Norman Blake • Kelly Joe Phelps • Cheryl Wheeler • Peter Mulvey • Dave Alvin • Steve James • Doc Watson • Eddie Lang • Jesse Winchester • Jesse Cook • Eliades Ochoa (CD-only bonus track)

64 pp., $16.95
Item #21699229
ISBN 1-890490-17-2

FLATPICKING GUITAR MASTERPIECES

Doc Watson • Norman Blake • Clarence White (Kentucky Colonels) • Dan Crary • Tony Rice • Mark O'Connor • Russ Barenberg • David Grier • Kenny Smith • Scott Nygaard • Bryan Sutton • Allison Brown

64 pp., $16.95
Item #21699260
ISBN 1-890490-32-6

HABITS OF THE HEART

Elliott Smith • Chris Whitley • David Grier • Guy Davis • Mike Dowling • Stephen Fearing • Laura Love • Josh White • Jerry Douglas • Merle Travis • Roy Rogers • Dan Bern • Kristin Hersh • Scott Tennant • Jim Croce

64 pp., $16.95
Item #21699182
ISBN 1-890490-16- 4

ALTERNATE TUNINGS GUITAR COLLECTION

David Wilcox • David Crosby with CPR • Sonny Chillingworth • John Cephas and Phil Wiggins • Ani DiFranco • Alex de Grassi • Dougie MacLean • Ledward Kaapana • Trian • Peter Finger • Mary Chapin Carpenter • Paul Brady

64 pp., $16.95
Item #21699239
ISBN 1-890490-27-X

HIGH ON A MOUNTAIN

Steve Earle and the Del McCoury Band • Wayne Henderson • Beth Orton • Franco Morone • Nick Drake • Kate and Anna McGarrigle • Clive Gregson • Woody Mann • Gillian Welch • Jones and Leva • Andrew York • Taj Mahal • El McMeen • Judith Edelman • Jennifer Kimball

72 pp., $16.95
Item #21699195
ISBN 1-890490-09-1

ACOUSTIC GUITAR ARTIST SONGBOOK, VOL. 1

Sérgio Assad • Duck Baker • Doyle Dykes • Steve Earle* • Beppe Gambetta • Vince Gill • John Wesley Harding • Michael Hedges* • Philip Hii • Robyn Hitchcock • Jewel* • Pat Kirtley • Earl Klugh • Mike Marshall • Pat Metheny • Keb' Mo'* • Scott Nygaard • Pierce Pettis • Kelly Joe Phelps • Chris Proctor • Andrés Segovia • Martin Simpson • Tim Sparks • Jorge Strunz • Toru Takemitsu • Townes Van Zandt • Gillian Welch • Paul Yandell

100 pp., 2 CDs, $29.95
Item #21699216
ISBN 1-890490-03-2

* Not included on CD

SHADES OF BLUE

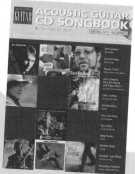

John Jackson • Paco Peña • Shawn Colvin • Dave Van Ronk • Barenberg, Douglas, Meyer • Ramblin' Jack Elliott • Bill Morrissey • Willy Porter • Kristina Olsen • David Lindley • Chris Smither • Honeyboy Edwards • Ben Harper (CD bonus track only)

64 pp., $16.95
Item #21699252
ISBN 1-890490-25-3

On every page of **Acoustic Guitar** Magazine, you'll recognize that same love and devotion you feel for your guitar.

Our goal is to share great guitar music with you, introduce you to the finest guitarists, songwriters, and luthiers of our time, and help you be a smarter owner and buyer of guitars and gear.

You'll also be getting the latest in gear news, artist interviews, practical player advice, songwriting tips, sheet music to play, music reviews, and more, every month.

Acoustic Guitar Magazine wants you to be happy. Let us show you how with THREE FREE issues. So subscribe now without any risk at the low introductory rate of $23.95 for 15 total issues, and enjoy three free issues compliments of *Acoustic Guitar* Magazine. You have our unconditional guarantee: You must be completely satisfied, or your payment will be refunded in full.

Three Free Issues!
Subscribe today
(800) 827-6837
Or, place your order on our Web site!
www.acousticguitar.com